CAMPUS CRUSA T5-ASQ-298

BIBLE CHARACTERS AND DOCTRINES

Paul's Friends to Caesar's Household

E. M. BLAIKLOCK, M.A., D.Litt.

The Mission of the Church

COLIN GRANT, B.Sc., B.D.

William B. Eerdmans Publishing Company
Grand Rapids, Michigan

CAMPUS CRUSADE FOR CHRIST LIBRARY

©1974 Scripture Union
First Published 1974
First United States Edition January 1975

Printed in the United States of America

Library of Congress Cataloging in Publication Data
Main entry under title:

Bible characters and doctrines.

   CONTENTS:
Cundall, A. E. God in His world. — v. 1.
Blaiklock, E. M. Adam To Esau. Crowe, P. The
God who speaks. — Scripture and revelation.
— v. 3. Blaiklock, E. M. Nadab to Boaz. Wright,
J. S. The character of God. [etc.]
   1. Bible — Study — Text-books. I. Blaiklock, E.
M. II. Wright, John Stafford. III. Grogan,
Geoffrey.
BS605.2.B47   220'.07   72-189855
ISBN 0-8028-1432-8 (v. 1)

SCRIPTURE UNION IN NORTH AMERICA
U.S.A.:   1716 Spruce Street
           Philadelphia, Pa. 19103
Canada: 5 Rowanwood Avenue, Toronto 5,
           Ontario

*All rights reserved. No part of this publication may be
reproduced, stored in a retrieval system, or transmitted
in any form or by any means, electronic, mechanical,
photocopying, recording, or otherwise, without the prior
permission of Scripture Union.*

Campus Crusade for Christ Library

BS
605.2
B582
v.14

INTRODUCTION

Each volume of Bible Characters and Doctrines is divided into the right number of sections to make daily use possible, though dates are not attached to the sections because of the books' continuing use as a complete set of character studies and doctrinal expositions. The study for each day is clearly numbered and the Bible passage to be read is placed alongside it.

Sections presenting the characters and doctrines alternate throughout each book, providing balance and variety in the selected subjects. At the end of each section there is a selection of questions and themes for further study related to the material covered in the preceding readings.

Each volume will provide material for one quarter's use, with between 91 and 96 sections. Where it is suggested that two sections should be read together in order to fit the three-month period, they are marked with an asterisk.

The scheme will be completed in four years. Professor E. M. Blaiklock, who writes all the character studies, will work progressively through the Old and New Testament records. Writers of the doctrinal sections contribute to a pattern of studies drawn up by the Rev. Geoffrey Grogan, Principal of the Bible Training Institute, Glasgow, in his capacity as Co-ordinating Editor. A chart overleaf indicates how the doctrinal sections are planned.

In this series biblical quotations are normally taken from the RSV unless otherwise identified. Occasionally Professor Blaiklock provides his own translation of the biblical text.

7759

DOCTRINAL STUDY SCHEME

	Year 1	Year 2	Year 3	Year 4
First Quarter	The God who Speaks	Man and Sin	The Work of Christ	The Kingdom and the Church
Second Quarter	God in His World	Law and Grace	Righteousness in Christ	The Mission of the Church
Third Quarter	The Character of God	The Life of Christ	Life in Christ	The Church's Ministry and Ordinances
Fourth Quarter	The Holy Trinity	The Person of Christ	The Holy Spirit	The Last Things

DOCTRINAL STUDIES
THE MISSION OF THE CHURCH

Study

The Missionary Purposes of God in the Old Testament

7	Boundaries of Blessing	Genesis 12.1–3; 22.15–18
8	Consequences of Election	Deuteronomy 10.12–19; 1 Kings 8.33–43
9	Conquests of Kingship	Psalm 2
10	Patterns of Righteousness	Isaiah 2.1–4; 11.1–10
11	Purposes of Grace	Isaiah 19
12	Characteristics of Christ	Isaiah 42.1–13; 49.1–7
13	Dissatisfactions of Idolatry	Jeremiah 16.14–21; Zephaniah 3.8–10
14	Patterns of Discipleship	Jonah 1 and 2
15	Principles of Mercy	Jonah 3 and 4

Mission and the Son of God

22	Focus of the Prophets	Luke 4.16–30
23	Seeker of the Lost	Luke 15
24	Saviour of the World	John 4.1–42
25	Friend of the Needy	Matthew 15.21–28
26	Shepherd of the Sheep	John 10.11–16; 11.47–53
27	Victor of the Cross	John 12.20–36

Mission and the Holy Spirit

36	Empowering for Mission	John 15.22–16.11; 20.19–23
37	Categories of Salvation	Luke 24.44–53
38	Enduement for Service	Acts 1.1–11
39	Experience of Promise	Acts 2
40	Crossing of Boundaries	Acts 8
41	Fulfilling of Prophecy	Acts 10
42	Establishing of Principles	Romans 15.7–21

5

Study

Mission and the Church

Paul the Missionary

Motive for Mission

CHARACTER STUDIES
PAUL'S FRIENDS TO CAESAR'S HOUSEHOLD

Study

Study

CHARACTER STUDIES

1: Paul's Friends
Acts 18.1–6; 1 Corinthians 2

Paul passed on to Corinth, possibly a prey to one of his periodic bouts of illness—if Ramsay is right in diagnosing the 'thorn in the flesh' as the debilitating malaria of coastal Asia Minor (1 Cor. 2.3; 1 Thess. 3.7). Paul was comforted by meeting two friends. Some disturbance in the Roman ghetto had led Claudius to expel the Jews from the capital. It was probably trouble connected with the first preaching of the gospel in the city. Hence the presence of Prisca (or Priscilla) and Aquila in Corinth. They were a much travelled pair. We find that they accompanied Paul to Ephesus where they instructed the preacher from Alexandria, Apollos (18.18, 24–26). Theirs was an open house. They returned to Rome when Claudius' decree was revoked, or became a dead letter (Rom. 16.3 f.). Again their home is a meeting-place for Christians. Aquila, observe (2), had been born in Pontus on the Black Sea. The couple played a noble part in the founding of European Christianity.

There is still a church of Saint Prisca on Rome's Aventine Hill, and there is a cemetery which bears her more affectionate and familiar name, Priscilla. This cemetery, William Barclay points out, was the burial ground of the ancient family of the Acilii, which gave Rome a consul, Acilius Glabrio, in A.D. 91, who seems to have died a martyr's death as a Christian five years later. If the Priscilla of the catacomb cemetery is the Priscilla of Acts, Aquila may have been a freedman of the family of the Acilii, an ex-slave, perhaps a Jew. Speculation, no more, but intriguing. And since Prisca is a common name of the Acilii, there could be in their partnership a moving illustration of the faith breaking through the barriers of caste and station, and uniting a Roman lady with a freedman of her house. It is a curious fact that in four of the six passages in which the pair are named, Prisca, contrary to custom, is named before her husband.

Paul needed friends. He was in another great Greek city, one of the most iniquitous places on earth. It was to be his triumph to plant the faith in its cosmopolitan streets. The home which the worthy couple provided was to be his refuge, his bridgehead and his shelter. Prisca and her husband played a vital part.

*2: The Corinthians

1 Corinthians 1

Paul recalled four years later that he had approached Corinth with some misgivings. He had spoken to the philosophers of Athens with deep understanding of their doctrine. This was, as we have seen, notably true of the Stoics. There were also aspects of Greek philosophy which he despised or actively repudiated and in Corinth Paul sensed a shallow intellectualism which made him determined not to preach the gospel in philosophic terms (1 Cor. 2.5), lest the truth which he desired above all else to stress should lose its impact and meaning. This is what the determination to 'know nothing else' (1 Cor. 2.2) but the simplicities of his message means. It is not a repudiation of the approach of the recent Areopagus address, but a demonstration of the writer's acute awareness of the peril of pandering to the pretentions of the Corinthian audience.

Corinth was not Athens—not Philippi, nor Tarsus. It was the most cosmopolitan of the cities of the Mediterranean, with the possible exception of Rome itself. Vicious, prosperous, without deep roots in tradition, the people of Corinth were too ready, with the facility of immigrant communities, to adopt the vices rather than the virtues of the land of their adoption, and to conform to Greek ways with little of deeper understanding. The letter deals with no fewer than five major problems—faction, morality, secularism, worship, and death. Philosophy, or what Corinth understood by that much tormented term, underlay all these problems. No common habit of thought gave the Christian group stability, coherence, and a form of unity, as it no doubt did in churches formed from synagogue communities. The Jews were probably a minority. There was no background of Scripture. The New Testament was hardly begun. The Old Testament had not the accepted authority which it had at Berea. Speculation, debate, conjecture were rife . . . It was, in short, a situation which has much to teach the modern world. For the first time since the first century, the world we live in is again a world of cities, with a mass of problems similar to those which confronted the Corinthians. Corinth might be London, New York, Sydney, where-ever this note is read. It is a sombre yet exciting thought.

*3: The Converts

Acts 18. 7–10

Paul's eighteen months of Christian preaching began in the synagogue but encountered again the fierce pride and nationalism of the Jewish minority, and the evangelist moved next door to the house of an adherent, one Justus. The rabbi of the synagogue came with him, a notable convert. The imperfect tenses of vs. 4 and 8 give an insight into Paul's patient teaching: 'He used to debate in the synagogue every Sabbath, and press his message on Jews and Greeks ... and many of the Corinthians who heard him would believe and be baptized.'

Paul felt deeply the vital nature of his task. Corinth was a cross-road of trade. From that point the faith could be disseminated down the sea-lanes of the world. He felt the urgency of the gospel on his heart. The brevity of time, the magnitude of the task, a sense of weakness, and withal of responsibility, all these, together with a consciousness of God's indwelling power, led to a change of method. Instead of reasoning (4) Paul now testified (5). Exactly what this means is difficult to say. Personal experience is certainly the keynote of the later speeches in the book of Acts. Perhaps 1 Cor. 2.1–4 refers to this simplification of his message.

The Corinthian Christians were a varied mixture. A few of the converts, some indeed 'wise men after the flesh' and 'noble' (1 Cor. 1.26), are known to us by name—Crispus, the ruler of the synagogue, Erastus, the city treasurer (Rom. 16.23; and perhaps Acts 19.22 and 2 Tim. 4.20), Stephanas and Gaius, who seem to have been in a position to exercise generous hospitality, and the lady Chloe, who had a large household. Also mentioned are Fortunatus, Achaicus, Quartus, and Tertius who acted as amanuensis for the Epistle to the Romans. A strong Latin element appears likely.

It was to prove a difficult congregation as the two letters to Corinth show. A Christian community tends to reflect the quali-ties and defects of the community in which it is located. The turbulence and spirit of faction, the fundamental scepticism, the deplorable relapses, the undue tolerance towards sins of impurity, the intellectual arrogance and philosophical posing, and the very abuse of the gifts of the Spirit for self-display, which seem to have marred the Christian community, were reflections of the life of the restless Greek city itself.

Paul, for all that, loved them and said some of his richest words to them. If the Corinthians could be welded into a Christian community, no congregation need despair.

4: The Proconsul

Acts 18.12–17

Junius Annaeus Gallio was the brother of the Roman philosopher and tutor of Nero, Lucius Annaeus Seneca. They were a Spanish family, two of many men, writers, senators, emperors, whom the great Romanized Iberian peninsula sent to Rome to be leaders in politics and culture. An inscription discovered at Delphi in 1905 indicates that Gallio was proconsul of Achaia in A.D. 52, thus providing a useful dating point for Paul's activities in Greece.

Gallio, according to the Roman poet Statius and also his brother Seneca, was a gentle and amiable person, and the Jews obviously misread both the magistrate and the situation. He was not the man to yield to noisy demonstrations and violence, a characteristic of such characters which not infrequently surprises those who seek to take advantage of what they imagine to be weakness. The Jews also thought to profit by the new magistrate's inexperience, and phrased their charge to look like one of treason. Perhaps, too, they forgot the fact that, with Claudius' expulsion of the Roman Jewish colony, the nation was somewhat under a judicial cloud, and not likely to obtain from the most impartial Roman court anything more than their bare due. Gallio proved quite capable of distinguishing, in spite of the ambiguous phraseology, between matters of serious political significance and matters relating to minutiae of Jewish law.

It is possible in Corinth to picture the scene. The old agora has been excavated with its row of shops overlooked by the remaining eight pillars of the temple of Apollo. The vast bulk of the acropolis, the Acrocorinthus, topped by the temple of Aphrodite, whose host of priestess-courtesans did much to give Corinth its rank flavour of moral corruption, stood high above the town. At the end of the market-place still stands the massive stone plat-form (the *bema*) on which Gallio sat, and in front the wide pavement on which the angry leaders of the synagogue crowded round their victim. There are few places where it is so easy to imagine the drama of the ancient scene. Paul must have met the magistrate's brusque intervention with some amazement. He had not even found it necessary to appeal to his Roman citizenship. As for the Jews, and Crispus' successor Sosthenes, their judicial unpopularity prompted the turbulent Corinthian mob to assault them. This was deplorable, but Gallio, annoyed at the pre-sumptuous and arrogant attitude of the synagogue, took no action.

5: Paul's Vow

Acts 18.18–23; 2 Corinthians 3.7–14; Galatians 3.23–28

The popular Scofield Bible, first published sixty-five years ago, heads this section of Luke's story sadly: 'The author of Rom. 6.14; 2 Cor. 3.7–14; and Gal. 3.23–28 takes a Jewish vow.' It is, in fact, a minor inconsistency difficult to reconcile in one so clear in his doctrine and so decisive in his way of life.

Cenchreae, the modern Kichries, lay some seven miles from Corinth on the Saronic Gulf. It was the great city's outlet to the Aegean Sea. Phoebe, who is commended to the Roman church, first of all the list in Paul's letter (16.1), came from Cenchreae, where a church functioned in her home. It was probably here that Paul found shelter during the period of his vow.

It was a Jewish ritual of gratitude to take a Nazirite vow. The whole proceeding is set out in Num. 6.1–21. Paul may have wished to thank God for the blessing and preservation he had known in Corinth. It may also have been prudent, after the ironical out-come of the prosecution in the proconsul's court, to withdraw from sight for a period of time, and Cenchreae was a convenient place of retirement. Nor, indeed, was a man with a shaven head without some salutary semblance of disguise. The normal pro-ceeding was to withdraw from the common pursuits of life for thirty days, while hair and beard grew again, to abstain from meat and wine, and in the end make certain offerings in the Temple.

The full story of what Paul had in mind eludes us. The con-venience of the Nazirite withdrawal has been noted, and there is

no doubt that, after his arduous time in Corinth, earning his own living and founding and instructing a church, the weary man needed rest and time for prayer and meditation. It may, on the other hand, have been a proceeding not without its peril. The sequel is perhaps found in a later chapter (**21.18–26**), where Paul is persuaded by the Pharisaic wing of the Church to demonstrate his continuing loyalty to Judaism by meeting the charges of four men who had undertaken precisely such a vow. The Jerusalem Christians, unsure of their Christian liberty, must have heard of Paul's act of compromise at Cenchreae, or observed its continuing evidence on his head, and seized upon it as a concession to them. It led to deep and serious trouble.

6: Apollos

Acts 18. 24–19.7; 1 Corinthians 3.1–6

The world's largest colony of expatriate Jews was in the great Egyptian city of Alexandria. Two-fifths of its million-strong population were Jews, rich, cultured, turbulent and powerful. A papyrus letter from the emperor Claudius, dated A.D. 42, rebukes both Jews and Gentiles for riotous behaviour, and seems to suggest that the trouble in the city was due to 'immigrants from Syria'—perhaps Christian missionaries.

The Jews of Alexandria, proud of their cultural and literary heritage, had given the world the Septuagint, the Greek version of the Old Testament. The Alexandrian synagogues were also the proponents of varied allegorical interpretations of the Old Testament, not unlike exaggerated forms of typology sometimes found in Christian contexts.

Apollos (the name is probably an abbreviation of Apollonius) was brought up in this tradition. He was accurately informed about Jesus, either by the 'visitors from Syria' mentioned in the memorandum of Claudius, or from some early written account—and the whole drift of papyrological study suggests that written information of this sort was of earlier date than was once thought possible. Apollos was a man of natural gifts and received the message with enthusiasm. He set out, in true Christian fervour, to propagate the truth he had discovered, and humbly received the deeper teaching given him by the devoted Priscilla and Aquila.

He moved from Ephesus to Corinth, where he showed a truly

Pauline ability in dealing with the informed Jews of the synagogue. There must have been in his teaching some characteristic features of Alexandrian scriptural interpretation for a group to gather round him, and exaggerate his distinctiveness, as the reference in the first Corinthian letter implies. Paul saw it as a genuine contribution to understanding—'Apollos watered'. Perhaps on the other hand the Corinthian faction had no centre in teaching but was merely a 'personality cult'. Apollos was eloquent, perhaps fervent in spirit, attractive ...

Perhaps Apollos' desire to dampen such unnecessary controversy lay behind his reluctance to return to Corinth, as Paul had requested (1 Cor. **16**.12). He was still active years later, and in Paul's confidence (Tit. **3**.13). The suggestion that he was the author of the epistle to the Hebrews is based on the allegorical exposition common in that book. It is a suggestion as old as Luther's days, but has no certain evidence to back it.

Questions and themes for study and discussion on Studies 1–6

1. The value of friendship in the Church.
2. Urban, suburban and rural Christianity.
3. The reflection of a community in the Church.
4. The law and evangelism in the modern world.
5. Paul and his vow.
6. Variety in evangelism.

THE MISSION OF THE CHURCH
Introduction

Despite all that has been written on the subject over recent years, evangelism and overseas missions are still frequently regarded as 'extracurricular activities' of the programme of the local church. Many Christians continue to believe that they have an open choice whether to become involved in these spheres of church life or not, and that there is little urgency or obligation accompanying the decision, one way or the other.

The result is that Christian witness to the neighbourhood and other areas of opportunity is largely neglected, the work of missionary societies and similar bodies lags through shortage of personnel and financial resources, and the concerned few are left to carry on as well as they can.

How different is the Bible's view of mission! From its pages, we are presented with the inescapable truth that mission, far from being an addition, should be the very expression of the life of the Church. We may summarize it as being *that activity of God through His Church whereby, in Jesus Christ, He calls men and women into fellowship with Himself, transforming the relationships between them and renewing society through them.*

'The coming of the Spirit made Christ's mandate (Matt. **28**.18–20) an organic part of the Church's being, and an essential expression of her life', writes Dr. Harry Boer in his memorable book *'Pentecost and Missions'*. The Christian thus becomes involved in mission not out of any extra 'choice' he may make but solely by reason of his personal commitment to Jesus Christ as Saviour and Lord. To try to 'opt out' or to 'prefer not to' is basically to deny the very foundation of one's personal experience of the Christian faith.

In this series we hope to develop this theme and show, among other things, that the Church's responsibility in mission rests not on two or three isolated texts but on the total pattern and mandate of Scripture. After examining some important Old Testament passages in the first section we will go on, in the next three sections, to study mission in its relation to Jesus Christ, the Holy

18

Spirit and the Early Church. To see mission personified, we will next look at the inner motivation and outward activity of Paul the apostle, and finally, in the sixth section, examine some Biblical motives for the task of mission.

For your background and further reading, the following books are recommended:

Evangelism in the Early Church by E. M. B. Green (Hodder and Stoughton)

Pentecost and Missions by H. R. Boer (Eerdmans)

The Ministry of the Spirit by Roland Allen (World Dominion Press)

For all the World by J. V. Taylor (Hodder and Stoughton)

One World, one Task by the Evangelical Alliance (Scripture Union)

Our Guilty Silence by J. R. W. Stott (Hodder and Stoughton)

Unchanging Mission by Douglas Webster (Hodder and Stoughton)

THE MISSION OF THE CHURCH

The Missionary Purposes of God in the Old Testament

7: Boundaries of Blessing

Genesis 12.1–3; 22.15–18

'Why did God choose so small and unknown a tribe as Israel for such special purposes? Why overlook the rest of the world?' are the frequently put questions. God's words to Abram, the father of Israel, make it abundantly clear that there was nothing parochial about the matter at all (12.2 f.; 22.18). God in His wisdom has committed Himself to human instruments in order to convey His blessings to the nations of the world. He has chosen men to reach men, and that was why He chose Abram. He needed a people to reach 'the peoples', and that was why in Abram He chose a nation, the nation of Israel. 'Election is for service. And if God chose Israel, it was not alone that He might reveal Himself to her but that He might claim her for service,' writes H. H. Rowley. She was selected, not because of her national grandeur or her numerical strength (Deut. 7.7), but because God has always chosen to reveal His glory through the few (1 Sam. 14.6; Luke 9.1) and the weak (2 Chron. 20.12; 2 Cor. 12.10).

Abram and his descendants were themselves, of course, to rejoice in a personal knowledge of God and an experience of His blessings (cf. 12.2; 22.17). But Abram was being taught that when God gives, He gives in over-flowing measure, so that there would be plenty available for others too! The variant renderings in 12.3 of 'shall . . . be blessed' (AV[KJV]) and 'shall bless themselves' (RSV) depend on the understanding of the use of the Hebrew verb as passive or reflexive; the New Testament application of the phrase (Acts 3.25; Gal. 3.8) would indicate the rightness of the former, though both are very similar in meaning. The phrases 'all the families of the earth' and 'all the nations of the earth' are symbolic of everything else in the Old Testament in relation to mission and foreshadow the great 'alls' of the New Testament (e.g. Matt. 28. 19; 1 Cor. 9. 22).

20

The principle of 'through *a* people to *all* the peoples' is central in the Biblical understanding of mission. Israel failed in great measure to fulfil her responsibilities in relation to it, and the Church has been very dilatory too. For Christians commitment to God is commitment also to His mission in all the world.

Abram's parish, as well as that of John Wesley, was the world. How big is yours?

8: Consequences of Election

Deuteronomy 10.12–19; 1 Kings 8.33–43

Israel were proud of the fact that they were 'the chosen people of God', but they had to learn that there was a clear 'requirement' (Deut. **10**.12) built in to this privilege. The first requirement was a whole-hearted devotion to God in terms of holy reverence, implicit obedience and loving service (Deut. **10**.12 f.). Here were the features of that distinctiveness which was meant to identify Israel among the people of the eastern Mediterranean lands and beyond.

Lest, however, such devotion should lead to the cultivation of a secluded form of piety, God emphasized to Israel that their godliness must be accompanied by a concern for others, particularly 'the sojourner' (Deut. **10**.19), the non-Israelite who had come to settle down among the people of Israel. Love for the sojourner stems firstly from God's own love for him (Deut. **10**.18, cf. Psa. **146**.9) and secondly from the fact that because Israel themselves were 'sojourners' in Egypt for 400 years (Deut. **10**.19, cf. Gen. **15**.13) they should realize only too well the need to understand and care for such people.

Included in the orbit of Solomon's prayer was another type of person, 'the foreigner' (1 Kings **8**.41 ff.). This term referred primarily to a non-Israelite living in his own country but which had also 'acquired a religious connotation because of the association of other nations with idolatry' (H. M. Carson). While God's main commands to Israel regarding 'the foreigner' concerned the need for a clear separation from his ungodly ways of life (e.g. Exod. **34**.11 ff.), Solomon visualized the occasion when a foreigner with a sincere desire to seek God and attracted by Israel's witness to Him would come to the fellowship of Israel

(42). Such would be an outstanding opportunity for God to reveal His concern for men beyond the borders of the Israelite nation and for Gentiles to be joined with Israel in worshipping the one, true God (43).

The world into which God sends us begins with 'the sojourner', the person living, studying, working, shopping, spending his leisure alongside of us. If we cannot witness effectively to 'the world where it begins' at this point, then it will be somewhat artificial to express interest in 'the foreigner' in 'the world overseas'. The Old Testament teaches us that genuine compassion will include both.

How many people are attracted to you because they have noticed God's power and presence in your life (cf. 1 Kings 8.42)?

9: Conquests of Kingship

Psalm 2

What a great Messianic Psalm this is! After the angry turbulence of the nations in rebellion against God (1–3), we are pointed to God's triumphant vindication of His sovereignty through the resurrection (cf. Acts 13.33) and enthronement (cf. Heb. 1.5; 5.5) of His Son (4–7). Notice that the enthronement of the Son is in special relationship to Mount Zion (6). This latter name was that originally given to the hill on which Jerusalem was built but at times was used to personify the people of God themselves (e.g. Psa. 97.8). This important truth of God's King enthroned for His people is seen in such New Testament verses as Eph. 1.22 and Matt. 28.18 f. where Jesus is declared to be 'head over all things *for the church*', and His supreme authority is the basis of the Church's mandate for world mission.

In the third major section of this psalm, (8–11) we 'overhear' the Father inviting His Son to request universal dominion with a view to exercising universal judgement (8 f.) and the whole of Scripture echoes with the fact that the request has been both made and answered (cf. Matt. 25.31 ff.; Rev. 11.15). Stemming from this declaration of universal sovereignty is an appeal to the kings and rulers of the earth to 'be wise', to cease from their raging and rebellion and turn to God in faith and submission. The Hebrew of vs. 11 and 12 is somewhat uncertain, but the rendering of the

RSV is as accurate as any. The concept of 'kissing the feet' as an expression of homage and worship may appear strange to Western ears, but is perfectly acceptable when seen against the oriental background of the Bible.

The appeal to men on the grounds of impending or future judgement is not an uncommon one in the Bible (e.g. Luke 3.7–9; Acts 17.30 f.). Have we today become so uncertain of the truth of divine judgement that we try to avoid the theme altogether? Jesus Christ is both Saviour of those who believe and the sovereign Judge of all men (John 3.16 f.; Acts 17.31). Our presentation of the gospel to the world will only be effective if it is in full accord with both of these truths.

How much do you 'see' Jesus Christ as King of kings and Lord of lords in today's world (cf. 2 Kings 6.17; Heb. 2.9)?

10: Patterns of Righteousness

Isaiah 2.1–4; 11.1–10

These two passages may be interpreted in varying ways. Some view them symbolically, relating them to the historic development of God's Kingdom among men. Others interpret them literally, applying them to a future 'millennial age' on earth. Yet others admit both of these interpretations, viewing the first as a partial and the second as a final fulfilment. A good deal depends on our general approach to Old Testament prophecy. Each must decide from his understanding of the rest of Scripture the interpretation that is the most satisfactory for him.

In the first passage, the exaltation of the Lord, represented by the elevating of His dwelling place high over the lesser peaks of human achievement and pride (cf. 12–16), is a precursor to the 'flowing' of the nations to Him (2) in order that they may hear God's Word and submit themselves to it (3). We note again that the testimony of the Lord to the nations is inextricably linked with His people in 'Zion'. A consequence of this submission of the peoples to God is a new standard of social righteousness, with hatred and warfare being displaced by love and peace in international relationships (4). The horizontal relationship of man with man is directly connected with the vertical relationship of man with God. Put the latter right, and the former is rectified too (cf. Luke 19.1–10; 1 John 4.20 f.).

The promised One of David's line, in the second passage, will be equipped for His ministry, not by inherited abilities, but by the endueing of the Spirit. This will give him three pairs of qualities necessary, in turn, for good government ('wisdom and understanding'), effective warfare ('counsel and might') and spiritual leadership ('knowledge and the fear of the Lord') (2). His ministry of judgement among men will be both just and decisive (4 f.), and relationships within the natural order will be transformed through Him (6 f., cf. Rom. 8. 19–23).

With all the interplay of detail in these two great Isaianic passages, the transforming effect of Messiah's rule in the hearts of men of all nations stands out. When He is present, nothing can be the same again. Because He is God indeed, men and nature yield to the power of His touch.

What are the most urgently needed directions for the social out-workings of the gospel in today's world?

11: Purposes of Grace

Isaiah 19

In this 'oracle', Egypt, Israel's deceitful and undependable Gentile neighbour (Isa. 20.1 ff.; 30.1 ff.; 31.1 ff. etc.), is scheduled for judgement, with its religion (1), unity (2), confidence (3), independence (4), natural resources (5–8) and rural industry (9 f.) feeling the impact of God's power. The whole nation is depicted as morally confused (11–15), and when God uses Israel in judgement against its peoples, they will 'tremble with fear' (16 f.).

Nevertheless, a 'yet more glorious day' is envisaged for Egypt, and how these words must have amazed those who heard them. In spite of Egypt's shady past and the deluge of judgement already predicted, God's purpose for this land will bring blessing not only to the nation but through them to the world. Isaiah sees the day when there will be a community who honour and serve Him within Egypt's borders (18). 'An altar to the Lord', the symbol of true worship, and a 'sacred pillar', a sign of declared allegiance and victory (Gen. 28.18 ff.; Exod. 24.4), will represent Egypt's

24

fidelity to God, who in turn, will make their cause His own in times of national emergency (19 f.). God will reveal Himself to Egypt, speaking in order to obtain a response of faith (21 f.) and wounding in order to heal (cf. Deut. 32.39).

That God would actually reveal Himself to Egypt must have been startling enough to Israelite ears. Even more amazing, however, would have been the news of future brotherhood and joint worship between Assyria and Egypt (23) with blessing flowing out to all the world from an Israel–Egypt–Assyria triumvirate.

Nothing could be clearer regarding the inclusion of the Gentiles within the purposes of God. This remains true, whether one views this passage literally, to be fulfilled at the end of time, or symbolically, seeing the conversion of Egypt and Assyria as representing the winning of the Gentiles in the gospel age. The terms 'the work of my hands' and 'my people', used of God's relationship with Israel (cf. Isa. 29.23; 60.21; Lev. 26.12; Ezek. 34.30), are now applied without qualification to Gentile peoples, making them, in Paul's words, 'fellow heirs, members of the same body, and partakers of the promise' (Eph. 3.6).

Is your witness being hindered by an incredulity about the possible conversion of some of your more 'hardened' workmates, neighbours or friends (cf. Acts 9.1–19)?

12: Characteristics of Christ

Isaiah 42.1–13; 49.1–7

These two passages are the first in a series of 'Servant Songs' in Isaiah (the others being found in 50.4–9; 52.13–53.12 and 61.1–4) in which the features of 'he who is to come' (Matt. 11.3) are clearly revealed.

The words 'my servant' are applied elsewhere by Isaiah to Israel as a nation (cf. 41.8 f.; 44.1 f.). The Hebrew mind easily gathered the plural into a personified singular; yet something much more than this is indicated in the Servant Songs. Here is someone who not only fulfilled but far exceeded all that the nation of Israel was meant to be and do.

The ministry of the Servant was firstly to be *unique in character* (42.1; 49.1 f.). The pronoun 'my' spells out an intimacy of relationship; God's purposes were to be clear to Him from birth, and His life was to be energized by God's Spirit (cf. Matt. 3.13–17). Secondly, His ministry was to be *global in extent* (**42**.1, 4; **49**. 1, 6). It was to be concerned with establishing 'justice' among men. This word, in this context, means 'true religion as a rule and law for life in all its relations' (Delitzsch). This ministry is to reach 'the nations', 'coasts and islands', 'peoples far away' and 'earth's farthest bounds' (NEB), and nothing could be more global than that (cf. John **10**.16)! In the third place, the ministry of the Servant was to be *exemplary in quality* (**42**.2 f.; **49**.2 f.). He would be no 'ranter', raucously peddling his verbal wares. He would be exquisitely tender among the bruised and flickering spirits of men, not harshly stamping on them as would others, but reaching out in love to reclaim and restore (cf. John **8**.1–11). Fourthly, the Servant's life would show a *tenaciousness in purpose* (**42**.4; **49**.4). With a Hebrew play on words, the writer pictures Him as not 'burning out' or being 'bruised away' until His goal is reached. The arrow of His life would hit the centre of the target, despite the apparently meagre reward for His labours (cf. John **1**.10–12; **17**.4). Finally, the Servant's ministry would be *enlightening in results* (**42**.6 f.; **49**.6). Darkness is a frequently used picture of the spiritual state of both Israel and the Gentile nations, and the Servant would bring the light of the knowledge of God to both (cf. John **8**. 12).

Little wonder that the peoples of the earth sing for joy and coastland settlers echo God's praise (**42**.10–12; cf. Psa. **96**.11 f.), and the breadth of the writer's outlook is again featured by the inclusion within his 'choir' of the Bedouin-type desert wanderers of Kedar, one of Israel's adversaries, and the Edomite dwellers of the rocky Sela plateau.

How much does our preoccupation with 'the machinery of mission' (e.g. its magazines, films or personalities) prevent us from being gripped by the glory of the Servant Lord of mission?

13: Dissatisfactions of Idolatry

Jeremiah 16.14–21; Zephaniah 3.8–10

Idolatry is a universal human tragedy. Because of the corruption and rebellion of his sinful heart, man basically refuses to worship and serve the God who made him and instead designs alternative objects for dependence and trust.

Jeremiah reminds Judah that the God who sees all (17) has observed their rebellious idolatry. The idols they adore are no better than carcasses, and as such defile the land (18). An idol is seen as an inheritance of 'sham' (19, NEB). Revered as true objects of worship, they are, in fact 'no gods' (cf. Psa. 96.5, where a Hebrew play on words identifies the nations' gods, *elohim*, as nothings, *elilim*, and 1 Cor. 8.4–6, where Paul contrasts 'so-called gods' with the one true God). There is no comparison between what they offer and the security God gives to those who 'from the ends of the earth' turn to Him (19).

A contemporary of Jeremiah, Zephaniah moves from the severe warnings of judgement for Judah and her neighbours, which have occupied him for most of his prophecy, to a vision of God's final judgement of the nations (8). His is the prerogative to 'gather' them for this purpose and the heat of His just reaction against their cumulated sin and rebellion will destroy the earth as well (cf. 2 Pet. 3.10 ff.). Yet, the outlook is not completely bleak. He who judges in righteousness is also He who acts in renewing power in men's hearts (9). The divisive judgement of Babel will be ended (Gen. 11.9) as the nations serve God 'with one accord'. 'Ethiopia' (the 'Cush' of the NEB is the transliteration of the Hebrew), one of the most distant of the nations known to Israel, symbolizes the worship the Gentiles will bring (10). Some scholars have seen a reference here to the regathering of a specifically Jewish dispersion, a common theme in the Old Testament (cf. Jer. 31. 10; Ezek. 11.7, etc.); the NEB with its 'my suppliants of the Dispersion' seems to assume it too. There is, however, no need for such a restricted interpretation.

What different forms does idolatry take among 'the nations' today?

14: Patterns of Discipleship

Jonah 1 and 2

Nineveh, the capital of Israel's last great enemy, Assyria, was the concentrated expression of heathenism and evil to the people of Israel. From this city, the Assyrian kings had vaunted their powers, campaigning for the nation's god, Ashur, and his many consorts, in order to subdue all who would not acknowledge his sovereignty. Against such a city, God commissioned Jonah for mission (1.1). Jonah, in his righteous disgust at the evil parade of the Assyrian capital, was basically unwilling to give any opportunity for God to have mercy on the city (cf. 3.10–4.2); for while God's mandate was indeed a message of denunciation (1.2), Jonah was well acquainted with the forgiving nature of the God he served.

With a mixture of shame and fear, both usually present when man disobeys God, Jonah headed for Tarshish, a trading centre on the coast of Spain and supposedly far away from the uncomfortable and demanding 'presence' of God. But the One who 'brings the wind out of His storehouses' (Psa. 135.7, NEB) and who made the sea and all it contains (cf. Exod. 20.11) exercised His sovereignty in both realms (1.4, 17). Even when God's servants disobey Him, they can never completely evade His all-embracing purposes for them and through the grace of God Jonah was soon being humbled before Him (1.12) and voicing thanksgiving to His Name (2.9).

The relationship of Christian disobedience to the fulfilling of the perfect will of God on earth is bound up in mystery. Centuries passed in the history of Christendom with the gospel being withheld from the world because of the denial of it by those who should have been sharing it. Even after the Reformation, the Church only slowly roused itself to take the gospel to all peoples and today much still remains to be done despite all that has been accomplished since William Carey arrived in India in 1793. Yet from our studies today and tomorrow, it will become quite clear that God in His wisdom, patience and grace, is able to gather up our human imperfection and still cause His goals to be attained and the ends of the earth to hear of His glory.

In relation to our disobedience in the task of mission, is this another case where 'the goodness of God' should lead us 'to repentance' (cf. Rom. 2.4)?

15: Principles of Mercy

Jonah 3 and 4

God spoke persistently and patiently 'the second time'. The servant of God had been chastened, but while his outward actions indicated obedience, his reactions afterwards (e.g. **4.1 ff.**) continued to show a grudging spirit. In Nineveh, the response was dramatic (**3.5 ff.**). God exercised His pardon (cf. Exod. **33.19**; Psa. **86.5**) and withheld His judgement (**3.10**). The use of the word 'repented' in **3.10** in relation to God implies, not, of course, a regret for previous or intended actions, but a sovereign change in His dealings with men in just accord with a new response and obedience on their part and in perfect harmony with His own nature.

To Jonah, the 'worst' had happened! Blatant evil had received mercy not judgement and it seemed as though God was allowing past evil to go unpunished. Jonah's failing was 'the sin of pretending to be more careful of God's glory and more qualified to advance it than God Himself' (Hugh Martin), and it led him to offer a confused prayer (**4.2 f.**) and to slink away under a cloud of self-embitterment (**4.5**). It may seem amazing to us that the repentance and pardon of ungodly men could lead to such a reaction, yet Jonah's aggrieved attitude was but a logical consequence of his basic unwillingness to obey God. Moreover, it was a reflection of the prevailing attitude within Israel as a whole at that time.

To show Jonah something of the religious exclusiveness that had been binding and blinding him, God spoke finally through an acted parable. Jonah's feelings at the withering of the gourd that had given him such valuable, if brief, protection were strong (**4.9 f.**). If Jonah could be capable of such deep emotion towards a mere plant that he had neither planted nor nourished, could not he begin to understand how greatly God Himself must care over an urban concentration of thousands of men and women whom He had created and who, in their ignorance, were in so much need of His pardon and true knowledge of Himself?

*Tokyo (12 million), London (8 million), Moscow (7 million), São Paulo (6 million). What is your attitude towards the people of such cities? (cf. Luke **13.34**).*

Questions and themes for study and discussion on Studies 7–15

1. 'Election has no goal in itself, but only the Kingdom of God' (C. Vriezen). How far does this summarize the Old Testament teaching on God's choice of Israel?

2. What do the final three 'Servant Songs' (see Study 12) teach on Christ's world-wide ministry?
3. What are the basic causes for disobedience among present-day Christians in their task of world-wide witness?

CHARACTER STUDIES

16: The Ephesians

Acts 19.23–41

The story of the riot in Ephesus is most interesting. It is a picture of a great ancient city in the days of its decline, difficult to match in surviving literature. Sir William Ramsay regarded it as a most revealing chapter, 'the most instructive picture of society in an ancient city which has come down to us . . . We are taken direct into the artisan life of Ephesus, and all is so true to common life and so unlike what would occur to anyone writing at a distance, that the conclusion is inevitable: we have here a picture drawn from nature.' The terse account reads, says Charles Seltman the classical scholar, who had no sympathy for Paul's 'puritanical' and Christian invasion of the Asian city, 'like a modern press report'.

The facets of life and history in the plain and well-told story are worth a closer look. The chief characters stand out—the two Macedonians, recognized as friends of Paul, and hustled down the street, whose marble paving still proclaims its elegance, on the wave of the moving horde; Paul, cool as ever in a crisis; the provincial custodians of the Caesar-cult, not sorry to see some damage to the religion of Artemis; Alexander, probably a Hellenistic Jew who was anxious not to be exposed to unnecessary unpopularity or pogrom because of the conduct of a splinter-sect . . . Observe too, the germs of coming conflict with the proletariat, which Tacitus and Pliny note in their first secular accounts of Christianity. The metrical chant is almost audible, as it takes the place of reason in the collective mind of an eastern mob, which Luke describes with a phrase of classic irony (32).

Observe too, the sure touch of Luke's plural, which slips into his report of the city-official's politic speech. 'There are pro-consuls' (38), he reminds the promoters of the tumult. Read this in the context of the speaker's anxiety over the privileged standing of his city, and another convincing mark of historicity appears. The plural conveys a touch of obsequious respect for the two imperial stewards, who, having murdered the proconsul of Asia,

31

M. Julius Silanus, the great-grandson of Augustus, must have been left with the administration of the province on their hands pending the appointment of a successor. The crime was of Agrippina's devising, shortly after her son Nero's accession in the autumn of A.D. 54. Tacitus takes occasion to make a bald account of it the preamble to his vivid narrative of Nero's principate. The tactful plural in the official's speech could then be evidence in one letter of the aftermath of political assassination. The Ephesian official is a clear-cut picture.

17: Sceva

Acts 19.8–22; Deuteronomy 13.1–5

Ephesus was a den of superstition. The worship of Diana, or Artemis of Ephesus to give the ancient Anatolian goddess her Greek name, was the occasion of a great pilgrim trade. It was a corrupt worship, that ultimate degradation of a nature-cult, with prostitute-priestesses in attendance for ritual obscenity. Amid the hordes who visited Ephesus were the superstitious, the seekers of sensation, and the motley host who, the world over and through all time, have been the provender of the charlatan, or the scamps who have battened on the vices and the folly of their fellows. Such villainy is not confined to ancient history. The holocaust of books on magic and allied superstition, which marked a genuine movement towards Christianity in the great pagan city (19), reveals the extent of the market which the writers of horoscopes, spells and charms could command among the cosmopolitan crowd. The city no doubt lived on such parasitic commerce, and this too is a situation not altogether unfamiliar in another city-ridden century. Pandering to vice and foolishness can prove rich gain. Sceva and his family were Jews who had seen the possibility of drawing financial advantage from the Christian movement. They were exorcists, who practised a base 'psychiatry' amid the unbalanced and the idly rich of the population. Observing the attraction which Paul's gospel was obviously manifesting, they thought to turn the name of Jesus to profit—with startling results.

As Jews their sin was doubly heinous. They knew well enough the denunciations of the Old Testament against the blasphemy of false prophecy. Sceva was a priest, and therefore of better than ordinary education in matters of Jewish religious concern. Not only was he prepared to deny and debase his own sacred calling, but he was careless of the spiritual well-being of his sons. A parent has touched the nether depths of sin when he deliberately communicates his wickedness to his offspring and initiates them into the practice of iniquity. Vice which seeks to propagate itself deliberately is a shocking spectacle, and no less horrifying is the evil which invades the holy place, and seeks, like Sceva's family, to enlist God in the quest of unclean gain.

18: Demetrius

Acts 19.23–32; Isaiah 40.12–26

Demetrius was a scamp of another sort. He too lived on a corruption of religion. The man stands out with some clarity in the terse account Luke writes of his rabble-rousing speech in the guildhall of the silversmiths. If an addition in the text of Acts in Codex Bezae is to be accepted, the place of meeting stood in the marble-paved street which sweeps up to the great theatre. Here is the speech as Luke gives it; it tells its own story:

'One Demetrius, a silversmith who made souvenir shrines of Artemis, provided plenty of work for his craftsmen. He gathered them together along with workmen in associated trades, and, addressing them, said: "Men, you are aware that our prosperity depends upon this business, and you see and hear that, not only in Ephesus but through almost all of the province, this Paul, by his preaching, has turned away a great host of people, telling them, as he does, that you cannot manufacture gods. Not only is our trade in danger of falling into contempt, but the temple of the great goddess Artemis will cease to be respected, and her majesty, whom all Asia and the civilized world worships, will be heading for destruction." When they heard these words they were filled with rage, and shouted: "Great is Artemis of the Ephesians." And the whole city was a scene of confusion. They surged with one accord to the theatre' (E.M.B.).

Note the familiar drift of the man's speech. He had a like-minded audience, and it is easy to produce, by inflamed rhetoric, a yell of approval from a crowd whose pockets have been similarly touched. The guild-master does not even trouble to put priorities in other than the obvious order. Trade is in danger from this new cult. Their livelihood depended on the silver souvenir

33

trade. Furthermore respect for Artemis will decline, and the respect is world-wide! The mob took the cue and began shouting for Artemis.

The object of this misguided and hypocritical loyalty was the Diopet—'the Thing Which Fell from Zeus'. It was probably a piece of meteoric iron or stone, perhaps bearing some semblance to a human figure and housed in the mighty temple. But here, in a vividly described incident of riot, demonstration and contrived disorder, is the full-length picture of a scoundrel who spear-headed a proletarian protest against the Church. It was to happen again in Bithynia in A.D. 111.

19: The Asiarchs

Acts 19.31; Ezra 1

The State is not always hostile to God's people. Ezra 1 reveals the favour shown by the Persians, who saw an ally for their comparatively lofty view of God in the Jews' religion. Something of the same preoccupation moved the 'rulers of Asia', or 'the chief men of Asia' to some show of friendship for Paul.

This honorary assembly was a body of substantial citizens who were called upon to finance public spectacles and games in the province of Asia. Perhaps such a festival was at the moment in train in Ephesus, with a vast influx of pilgrims and tourists providing more ample fuel for Demetrius' fiery speech. In such a case the presiding Asiarchs would be most reluctant to have their great occasion spoiled by a riot in the city. The Roman government, by whose grace and favour they held the honour, was most sensitive to any disturbance of the peace, and Ephesus, as a so-called free city, was notably anxious to avoid all cause of offence to the imperial authorities.

Asiarchs were elected for a term (it is not certain whether it was four years or less) and when the term expired, the incumbent of office retained the honorary title permanently. It might be that several such men lived at Ephesus, and that, seeing they were, among other duties, the presiding priests of the imperial cult, the formal worship of the spirit of Rome and the Empire which was later to occasion the disastrous clash between State and Church, they were not sorry to see the rise of any religion which weakened the influence of the prevailing cult of the Ephesian Artemis.

It may therefore be guessed that the Asiarchs passed a word of warning to Paul, not so much out of acceptance or regard for his message, as because they approved of the social consequences of his activities. The Christian sometimes finds friends in unexpected places. It may be also true that they added a word of advice to leave the city, and not risk further mob action on the part of the silversmiths. Paul seems to make a fairly prompt withdrawal across the Aegean. A strong church had been founded, and of that church we are to hear more in the later pages of the New Testament. Paul was becoming accustomed to such retreat.

20: Eutychus

Acts 20.1–16

We select one obscure and unknown character from several crowded months of evangelistic activity. Even a plot against Paul's life is passed over in a verse (3). We get a brief picture of the church at Troas, its communion service, and the evening sermon. Paul was no half-hour preacher, in spite of the fact that his congregation gathered after working hours in a crowded upper room of the house.

The poor lad Eutychus tried hard to keep awake. He found a window, open to the night air, high in a wall, and sat there in an attempt to breathe the stimulating air. His calculations miscarried, for the smell of the burning oil-lamps and the heavy air rose, and increased the boy's malaise. He dozed and fell into the street from the window alcove. Curiously enough, a second century papyrus from the days of Marcus Aurelius, contains the report of just such an accident. A little slave-boy, named Epaphroditos, eight years old, leaned out of a high window to see some dancers in the street of Oxyrhynchos, and fell to his death.

Luke was a physician, and perhaps that is why he picks this one incident from a crowded period. (The pronoun 'we' [7] shows that he was in Paul's company again.) The story is told with the reserve which might mark swift action to restore life in an emergency in a hospital or some scene of accident. Luke appears to vouch for the lad's death, though Paul retains hope of restoration. There is no contradiction, apart from miraculous intervention. Paul's prompt command of the situation is again apparent. In a surge of agonized concern, Paul's faith and action rose to the tragic occasion and the lad's life was restored.

The meeting continued, sustained by the passionate interest of Christians who had no New Testament. It went on till dawn was breaking over Mount Ida. Paul did not sail with them when they left. He wanted to walk alone across the headland by the old Roman road to Assos in Mysia. Did he dislike the thought of a stormy voyage round Cape Lectum? Did he stay behind to see how Eutychus fared? Had he heavy preoccupations or problems, and wanted to be alone to think? We do not know.

21: Ephesian Elders

Acts 20.17–38; Ezekiel 3.15–21

Luke reports in this moving passage the only speech of Paul in his book which it is certain he actually heard. Usually he reports in outline, probably from Paul's description or Paul's notes. Here he is setting down words which he actually heard, and it is interesting to note how he uses Pauline expressions found in the letters. In consequence the speech authenticates the epistles and the epistles the speech. R. B. Rackham, in his fine commentary on Acts develops this theme, but those who find such authentication interesting could look in sequence at the following list of echoes in the text: Rom. 1.1; Phil. 1.1; Tit. 1.1; 2 Cor. 2.4; 1 Cor. 10.33; 2 Tim. 4.7; 1 Tim. 1.12; 1 Cor. 11.23; 2 Cor. 7.2; Col. 4.17; 1 Tim. 4.16; Eph. 1.14; 2 Tim. 4.5; Col. 1.12, 28.

The words are vivid. Verse 19 is Paul's picture of himself. 'The narrative in Acts,' writes A. W. F. Blunt, 'has told us nothing of "tears"; it pictures Paul as the man who is always equal to a public emergency; Paul himself knows more of the private depressions and discouragements which he had to live through.'

There is also a clear picture of the three years in Ephesus. Paul sought no cheap popularity. Set like Ezekiel to the task of a watchman, he did his duty with zeal and consistent testimony. Note his tireless evangelism. Publicly and from house to house he had preached the gospel and founded Christian communities, not only in Ephesus but in the inland valley towns of Thyatira, Pergamum, Laodicea, Sardis, Philadelphia, Colossae and Hierapolis, as well as in the port of Smyrna. He lived in sturdy independence, earning his own bread. And with clear foresight he saw the shape of the troubles which John's letters to the seven churches (Rev. **2** and **3**) show truly came. He left the church efficiently organized and, as far as human organization could guard against trouble, he left constituted leaders, duly warned and strengthened against subversion, to meet and solve problems yet to be.

It seems clear from the fact that Paul met the elders of Ephesus on the Miletus beach that he no longer had access to the city. The sailing programme of the ship may of course have precluded a visit but it is as likely that the Asiarchs had suggested that abstention from future intrusion might add to his safety and minimize their own problems.

Questions and themes for study and discussion on Studies 16–21

1. Does Christianity still embarrass commerce?
2. Commercializing religion.
3. The art of rabble-rousing, the 'demonstration', and the Christian attitude.
4. Courage and prudence in the face of danger.
5. Luke's brevity and expansiveness.
6. Paul's warning to the Ephesians.

THE MISSION OF THE CHURCH

Mission and the Son of God

22: Focus of the Prophets

Luke 4.16–30

This incident could be quite separate from that recorded in Matt. **13**.53–58 and Mark **6**.1–6, or Luke might have brought it ahead of its exact chronological placing because of its excellent symbolic introduction to the ministry of Jesus that he was to tell. In reading verses from the prophets, our Lord responds to the usual invitation given to a travelling rabbi (cf. Acts **13**.15 ff.) after the prescribed portion from the law had been read by one of the resident teachers of the synagogue. Jesus reads from Isa. **61**.1–4 (probably the fifth of the 'Servant Songs'), the minor modifications we notice in the Gospel account being the result of Luke's dependence on the Septuagint and the incorporation by our Lord of an additional phrase, reflecting Isa. **58**.6, which further enlarges on the ministry of 'The Servant' in liberating the oppressed among men. He who could say of the Scriptures 'Their testimony points to me' (John **5**.39, NEB, cf. 1 Pet. **1**.10–12) leaves His hearers in no doubt as to the One about whom Isaiah was writing (21)! He would be the instrument both for effecting as well as for proclaiming the long awaited New Age when God would grant deliverance to men in a way hitherto unparalleled in human history.

Anticipating the eventual rejection by His hearers of both Himself and His claim, He shows that when faced with similar rejection and unbelief from Israel, both Elijah and Elisha were used in blessing to Gentiles (24–27, cf. 1 Kings **17**.8–16; 2 Kings **5**.1–14).

No wonder the sensitive Jewish audience was 'infuriated' (28, NEB) and took measures to kill Him (29 f.)! In the succeeding months and years, it was to be seen that the global bounds of the Old Testament Scriptures were the very categories that would characterize His own ministry and that of His Church. The responsibility for making known the glory of God in the world, a task in which Israel had so tragically failed, would be uniquely fulfilled in Him; whatever the consequences, He would not be party to the false parochialism of His fellow-countrymen.

*Are we too institutionalized and 'respectable' to mix sufficiently with people **where they are** so that Christ can 'announce good news' and 'set captives free' through us today?*

23: Seeker of the Lost

Luke 15

The immediate occasion for much of our Lord's teaching was the need to minister to those who misunderstood and criticized Him. The set of three parables we study today comes within this grouping (cf. 1 f.). To the Jew, 'a sinner' was both one who lived an openly immoral life and one who followed a dishonourable calling (see *The Parables of Jesus* by Joachim Jeremias). The eagerness of such people to hear Jesus stood out in stark contrast to the offended pride of the Pharisees. As we see our Lord welcoming 'sinners', we realize that His attitude 'is no mere humanitarian enthusiasm . . . but the manifestation of the will and purpose of God' (T. W. Manson).

The first two parables (4–7; 8–10) with their ancillary lessons of persistent and patient seeking for that which is lost, point us primarily to 'the redemptive joy of God'. It is this joy in which the Pharisees ought to have been sharing rather than being soured through their proud self-righteousness. Pharisees were, of course, prepared to welcome the repentant sinner if the latter would come to them. Jesus showed them that the love of God is of a different quality altogether.

In our traditional focus on 'the Prodigal Son' of the third parable (11–32), we have tended to overlook that the story is more properly geared to teach us primarily about 'The Loving Father'. His watching, waiting love surges forward in a run, an embrace and a royal welcome when the repentant son of the family returns. Here was no cool and calculated response, such as could be expected from the Pharisees; and there was certainly no semblance of that grudging 'stand-offishness' shown by the second son of the family, in whom the Pharisees were meant to detect their own image. The hardness of their own hearts is crushingly demonstrated in the parable's depiction of the Father being ready to 'go out' *to his eldest son also* in order to reason with him regarding his attitude (28).

When love is not prepared to spend itself in seeking the lost of its neighbourhood, whatever may be the cost in time, personal convenience and public esteem, and when love becomes so formalized that the repentant sinner is just another notch on a 'church growth' report, then that 'love' is 'good for nothing' and becomes mere noise (Matt. 5.13; 1 Cor. 13.1).

24. Saviour of the World

John 4.1–42

During His direct journey from Jerusalem to Galilee (3 f.), Jesus took the opportunity of His meeting with the Samaritan woman (cf. *New Bible Dictionary* on 'Samaritans') to minister to her need. In so doing, He set aside the traditional Jewish prejudices of sex and race in such a situation, and foreshadowed the bringing of the gospel to the people of that land by the early Christians (cf. Acts 8.1) and by Philip in particular (cf. Acts 8.5 ff.). After His offer to her of 'living water' (7–15), the woman recognized something of our Lord's spiritual stature through His exposure of her life (16–18). She hastened to turn the conversation away from herself to the question of the respective merits of Mount Gerizim, the Samaritan centre of devotion, and Jerusalem as suitable locations for the worship of God (20). The reply of Jesus states the basic principle that true worship is not a question of correct geography but of correct spiritual understanding (21–23). The dawning of God's New Age would indeed come from preparatory revelation possessed by the Jews, and not from the Samaritan's partial and confused patterns (22); but because the true God is 'spirit' (not 'a spirit' as in AV [KJV]), those who worship Him must possess corresponding qualities of heart (24). Such, whether they be in Borneo, Brazil, Britain or Burundi, will, if the focus of their faith is Jesus Christ, 'the truth', be accepted (cf. John 14.6; Mal. 1.11; Acts 10.35). Such will never be cast out (cf. John 6.37).

As a result of the woman's eager testimony (28 ff.), the first fruits of the spiritual harvest among the Samaritan nation were gathered (39, 41). The testimony of these new believers was to One whose blessings of salvation were not for the Jews only but for them also, representatives as they were of 'the world' (42).

Jesus used such a time of spiritual reaping to urge on His disciples the need to take advantage of every immediate opportunity to do God's will among men and not to remain inactive in the mistaken belief that 'the time is not yet ripe' (35 f.). He Himself had just given them an unforgettable example of how to minister 'in season and out of season' (2 Tim. 4.2).

Is your church guilty of awaiting 'a suitable season' to minister to its neighbourhood?

25: Friend of the Needy

Matthew 15.21–28

To the Jew, the Phoenician coastal towns of Tyre and Sidon (21) 'were not places where Messianic works were destined to be performed' (R.V.G. Tasker, cf. 11.21). Yet Jesus once more takes the opportunity to minister to another Gentile woman whose people followed a popular religious blend of polytheism and fertility cults. 'In the background was her religion, in the foreground was her need,' writes G. Campbell Morgan. Her lips express the cry of a mother's aching heart (22) to the visiting 'Son of David', of whose fame she had no doubt heard (cf. 4.24).

Our Lord's initial reluctance to help her (23, 26) was an expression of His prior sense of purpose to those who, of all peoples, should have been prepared for His coming (cf. 10.5 f.; Rom. 15.8 f.). For this reason, He was unwilling to become caught up during His earthly life in a large scale mission among Gentile people. His statement of intent (24), however, did but evoke an open-hearted plea, urgent in its simplicity (25, cf. 14.30). Our Lord's reply (26) 'was not a simple monosyllabic negative . . . but an argument inviting further discussion' (A. B. Bruce), with the word used in vs. 26 f. for dog *kunarion* being the diminutive form meaning the household dog rather than the savage 'pariah' of the streets. The woman assents to the principle (27) and with a blend of humility, humour, faith and spiritual insight presses her plea.

Once before, Jesus had occasion to marvel at a Gentile's great faith and on that occasion too He had healed at a distance (28; **8.**5–13). Against the hostility of Jewish officialdom, such 'faith active in love' (Gal. **5.**6, NEB) must have been refreshing indeed! God's Spirit moves in what are often, to our eyes, the most unexpected of places and the most surprising of people. Yet, far from being taken unawares, we should be serving and praying in anticipation of just this (cf. Isa. **65.**1).

Genuine faith wherever it appears is always 'given' faith (cf. Acts **14.**27; *Eph.* **2.**8).

26: Shepherd of the Sheep

John 10.11–16; 11.47–53

Jesus, the Good Shepherd, proves the genuineness of His credentials not only by fidelity to His flock, even to the sacrifice of His own life on their behalf (**10.**11–15), but by His compelling purpose to gather those 'sheep' still outside of His fold (**10.**16). The AV (KJV), by too much dependence on the Vulgate, disguises the two separate Greek words used in v. 16 for 'fold' (*aulē*) and 'flock' (*poimnē*), cf. RSV and NEB; 'the sheep not of this fold are non-Jewish Christians. Only when all that are Christ's, in whatever fold they may be found, have responded to the gospel will the ideal of one flock under one shepherd be a reality' (R. V. G. Tasker). The 'must' of Christ impelled Him not only to seek and save the lost during His earthly years (cf. Luke **19.**10) but to offer His life in a substitutionary death, planned so cruelly by the unscrupulous political manoeuvrings of Caiaphas (**11.**50) and yet centred so surely in the sovereign purposes of God (**10.**17 f.; Acts **2.**23). This death would form the basis for the world-wide 'gathering' that was to follow, in which Jew and Gentile alike would find personal relationship with God (**11.**52, cf. **1.**12; Gal. **3.**26 ff.).

The misguided conservatism of the Jewish leaders would have denied that God had a redeeming purpose for any fold outside that of Judaism. Even some in the Early Church at first insisted that a Gentile should be 'in Israel' as well as 'in Christ' (cf. Acts **15.**5; Gal. **2.**4 ff.). No wonder the Spirit of Truth had to shatter such views (cf. Acts **15.**19 ff.; Gal. **3.**1 ff.)! In view of the Church today having lost so much of that dynamic mobility for 'seeking' and 'gathering' that should characterize its life, one of its paramount needs is a similar 'shattering' experience from the Holy Spirit.

If you would have Jesus as the Good Shepherd to lead you 'beside still waters' (Psa. 23.2), you must have Him also as the One who, through you, 'must bring' the lost to Himself (10.16), whatever the cost (cf. 15.18 ff.).

27: Victor of the Cross

John 12.20–36

'The world has gone after Him,' scoffed the Pharisees (19), but the universal appeal of Jesus was illustrated far more effectively than they actually desired through the earnest enquiry of the Greek proselytes in Jerusalem for the Passover Feast (20 f.)! Our Lord was aware that 'His hour' (23, 27, cf. 2.4; 7.30, etc.) was upon Him, and as part of 'the glory' of it, He saw 'the rich harvest' (24, NEB) that would follow His being 'sown in the ground' through death. The coming of the Greeks was a first fruits of that greater turning to Him from the Gentile world which was the hope of all Scripture and of which He had already spoken (cf. 10.16).

Jesus was deeply conscious of all that would be involved in the Cross. He contemplated the hypothetical alternative of requesting His Father to save Him from (Gk. *ek* out of) it all (27), yet He refused it immediately with a firm 'No' (cf. Matt. 26.39). The whole course of His life lay in the direction of Calvary, and He had repeatedly rejected the Evil One's subtle overtures to follow an easier but defeatist path (Matt. 4.8 f.; 16.22 f.). These initial victories were portents of that greater victory over Satan which would be gained at the Cross itself when he, 'the ruler of this world' would be 'ejected from his dominion' (Marcus Dods) and deprived of his power to hold the hearts and wills of men in thraldom (31, cf. 16.11). The decisive nature of Christ's death at the Cross interpreted as a victory over the powers of evil is continued throughout the New Testament and forms the basis for our Lord's right and power to 'draw all men' to Himself (32, cf. 6.44 where the same verb *helkō* is used).

How are we to interpret the 'all' in this verse? If it means 'all without exception', then we are faced either with a universalistic interpretation whereby 'all will eventually be saved', a line of teaching contrary to Scripture as a whole (cf. Matt. **25**.46; John **3**.36; Rev. **20**.11 ff.), or with the need to read it with the sense of drawing to salvation *and* to judgement, an idea which 'cannot be excluded in view of v. 31' (Donald Guthrie). It would seem better, however, to see 'all' as meaning 'all without distinction', men from every nation, whether they be Jew or Gentile, African or European, Buddhist or Moslem, educated or illiterate, rich or poor. This reflects not only the thought of several other passages in John's Gospel (e.g. **4**.39 ff.; **10**.11 ff.) but also the trend of Scriptural teaching as a whole (Acts **10**.34; Rom. **3**.21 ff.; Rev. **5**.9, etc.).

How much time do you give each week to reading or hearing about 'the drawing power of Christ' among the peoples of the world?

Questions and themes for study and discussion on Studies 22–27

1. 'It is not enough to be told that God loves; the reality of love lies in a region other than that of words' (James Denney). How did this apply to the ministry of our Lord?
2. Among the varieties of religious experience in the world, what are the places where true spiritual need is personally felt?
3. Where is the victory of the Cross to be seen in today's world?

CHARACTER STUDIES

28: Philip's Daughters

Acts 21.1–9; 1 Corinthians 13.8–13

It is interesting to follow the course of the ship on a map. It was a frequented sea-lane, which was determined by the direction of day-time winds, a meteorological pattern itself dictated by the contours of the great land mass of Asia Minor and the contiguous sea. It was a route mentioned by two first-century Roman writers, and was probably full of ships. It took seven days to unload the galley at Tyre, where Paul may have seen the mosaic-paved shopping street, where Jesus could have walked on His one journey to the north. It is visible today.

Indefatigably Paul sought out the church, and was warned not to go to Jerusalem. It seems difficult to avoid the conclusion that Paul was moving against the revealed will of God in his determination to carry the monetary evidence of the Gentile Christians' goodwill to the Jerusalem church. Great and good men, in the grip of a fixed idea, can err.

The great galley unloaded, and moved on to Akko (Ptolemais), and the large Herodian port of Caesarea, where Philip had long been in residence. It must have been on this occasion that Luke talked with the evangelist, and heard the story of Candace's officer, which he recorded in Acts **8**. Always interested in the part women played in the Church, he noted the fact that Philip had three unmarried daughters active in the Christian ministry.

To 'prophesy' is to preach. Jeremy Taylor's work on 'The Liberty of Prophesying' was written, not to uphold the liberty of prediction, but freedom to preach and proclaim the message of the gospel. Such was the wider Elizabethan use of the word. In the New Testament the 'prophet', as distinct from the teacher, seems to have been a person of insight into spiritual truth. The teacher worked within the borders of established and approved doctrine. Hence the meaning of Paul's remark to the Corinthian church about the end of prophecy, as the ancient world knew it. He was pointing out that, when the full corpus of Christian doctrine was complete, there would no longer be an office for the person whose prime duty was to show new facets of truth. To be sure, in a lesser sense, the prophet has always been active. There are infinite varieties of presentation of the faith and its significance. It may no longer be basically expanded or diminished. It may be no longer reshaped, only infinitely applied.

29: Agabus

Acts 21.10–17; Jeremiah 13.1–11

Into the quiet household at Caesarea where Paul found refuge, came the strange person about whom we first read in chapter 11. He was shaped on the model of an Old Testament prophet. The three greatest Old Testament writing prophets used symbolism and object-lesson to drive home some spiritual truth, and Agabus carried a warning which must have had a strong impact on a man of Paul's training.

It convinced the congregation at Caesarea (12), who were loud in their entreaties. After all, apart from the alarming character of Agabus' warning, he knew Jerusalem and its tense atmosphere, for the passions which, a few years later, broke into the conflagration of the great rebellion of Jewry, were already hot in the air. Paul was known as a declared Roman citizen. His work among the Gentiles was considered by some a betrayal. A plot against his life had already been foiled. Luke himself added his plea ('we' in v. 14 shows that he supported the general warning).

Paul's determination to persist in the course of danger is puzzling. Perhaps he sought to follow the steps of Christ's passion and His 'setting His face steadfastly to go to Jerusalem' (Luke 9.51). Some deep inner compulsion moved him, and it is not for anyone to question the validity of such conviction in the case of another. At the same time, it is certainly a fact that a good man, unable to face objectively the nature of his motives, can be lamentably wrong. On the face of it, Paul seems to have moved on against unanimous, wise, loving and sincere advice, and commonly such counsel can be regarded as a major factor in the guidance of God. Scripture never hesitates to record a failing or a weakness in a noble man, and it is difficult to believe that Luke did not deplore his friend's determination. It is quite certain that a mighty ministry was to be tragically abbreviated by the events which the visit to Jerusalem precipitated. On the other hand, the custody of Paul produced the work of Luke, even if it did silence for vital years the potent preaching of Paul. Good can be drawn from error, if error be committed to God, and Paul's voice rings in the writings of his friend.

30: Jerusalem Church

Acts 21.15–26; 1 Corinthians 9.19–23

Luke remarks that the Jerusalem church received Paul and his party with warmth (17), and they no doubt took over, at some official reception, the considerable sum of money which Paul brought from the Gentile congregations. Luke says no more and it is a fair guess that the meeting proved to Paul a bitter disappointment. On the other hand, Luke is in one of his abbreviating phases, and the narrative, moving swiftly on to more vital events may disguise a time lapse which absolves James, the undisputed leader of the Jerusalem church, of any charge of a suspicious and unworthy attitude towards Paul.

The Jerusalem leaders could have been in a difficult position. In the Jerusalem Conference (Acts 15) they had gone as far as they could to conciliate the Gentile congregations. Ten years had passed. Such liberalizing influence which men like Peter, Barnabas and others might have exercised was weakening, as missionary activities abroad withdrew such leadership from the mother church. The Gentile church was growing more and more powerful, and the Jewish church in Jerusalem, a continual scene of Pharisaic and Judaizing activity, was probably growing narrower and narrower amid a resurgent Jewish nationalism. The atmosphere of the capital was becoming heavier each year with the menace of coming rebellion against Rome, and it is difficult for any congregation to escape the influence of its time and place. The Jewish tide was rising. Hence the suggestion, almost an order, from James. The Gentiles, he hints, had won a great concession. Why should Paul not yield a little, and demonstrate publicly that his now famous ministry among the Gentiles had not destroyed his old Jewish loyalties. It was a little thing, and had they not heard that he himself had made such a vow in Cenchreae, and had he not written of his willingness to be 'all things to all men if by any means he might win some'?

Paul, agonizingly anxious to win his old associates, conceded the point. It was a magnanimous second mile, but, as it turned out, a disastrous mistake. He was not to know that within a decade the stiff-necked Jerusalem church would cease to exist. He was weary of conflict. He sought to love and understand—and failed.

31: The Crowd

Acts 21.26–40

The riot in the temple court, entirely the fault of the unwise advice given to Paul, is told in fine terse prose, obviously the narrative of an eyewitness. Paul's old enemies from Asia had been overlooked in the apostle's eagerness to meet the wishes of the Christian Pharisees. Ephesus had already demonstrated the possibilities of mob violence, and the peculiarities of crowd-psychology. It appeared again.

There is cruelty in all primitive forces. Wind and wave and fire can be ruthless. So can the gales of emotion which sweep through crowds and peoples, turning groups of human beings into destroying hordes. Crowds tend to reflect the morality of their basest elements. They act in mass ignorance, as Luke remarked of the Ephesian mob (19.32). As Gustave Le Bon said at the beginning of the century: 'The individual forming part of a crowd acquires, solely from numerical considerations, a sentiment of invincible power, which allows him to yield to instincts, which, had he been alone, he would perforce have kept in check.'

Crowds, in consequence, lack self-consciousness and any sense of responsibility. They are prone to be carried away by a feeling of power, in which the individual, losing name and identity, lends himself to deeds of evil. The Romans feared the Jerusalem mob, and had good reason to do so. It was to be just such a mad riot which, in A.D. 66, would spark off the terrible four years of the great Jewish rebellion.

Crying havoc against Paul, the Ephesian group stirred such a tumult that the garrison, stationed in the Tower of Antonia overlooking the area, was alerted and driven to intervention. A strong patrol descended one of the two stairways which led to the area, and drove violently through the crowd to the rescue. The impression was that a Jew from Egypt, a member probably of the notoriously riotous Alexandrian ghetto, was at his rabble-rousing again.

Holding the crowd at bay, the tough soldiers carried Paul off with the old familiar cry of the Lord's passion ringing: 'Away with him . . .'

32: Lysias and Paul

Acts 22

The tribune in charge of the garrison, Claudius Lysias, appears to have been one of the career men frequently met in the days of Claudius' two notorious freedmen ministers, Pallas and Narcissus. He was a Greek, as his second name indicates, and his first name was acquired when, at the price of a considerable bribe, a piece of corruption common enough in that venal group, he was granted the still coveted Roman citizenship. On the other hand Lysias seems to have been a vigorous and capable soldier, with good relations with his staff (26). The centurion is at ease with his commander.

Obviously Paul made a strong impression on the Roman officer. He did not reveal his Roman citizenship until after the second outburst of mob rage, and it says something for the commanding personality of the prisoner that a senior officer paused in the midst of a tense and perilous operation, and allowed an unidentified prisoner, just snatched by force from the hands of a wildly excited mob, to stand on the stairs which led to the security of the tower, and, over the narrow barricade of the soldiers' spears, address the seething crowd below. We have remarked that Paul was the first European, the first character of whom history has clear record, who bore in his own person the integrated heritage of the three cultures from which European civilization has sprung. It was his speaking Greek which first caught the attention of the Roman tribune. He addressed the crowd in their Hebrew dialect. He was soon to claim his Roman rights and win them.

It was also on Paul's part a remarkable exhibition of cool courage and superb self-control. He had just been saved from lynching by the intervention of a rough detachment of soldiery, men who probably took little care to be gentle with the person at the centre of the disturbance. Most people would be too shaken by their grim experience to be able to stand and speak coherently, as Paul quite obviously did. He seized the opportunity to testify, and, in spite of the violence of which he had just been the victim, did all he could to conciliate the crowd. He postponed as far as possible any reference to Gentiles, even at one point (15), modifying Christ's words to do so. The spirit of the mob is revealed by the explosive power of this one word (22).

33: The Sanhedrists and Paul

Acts 23.1–11; Matthew 26.57–66

Snatched into the safety of the fort, Paul, no doubt, faced trouble with Lysias, who probably knew no Aramaic, and may have regarded the new outbreak of protest as a poor return for the concession he had granted his remarkable prisoner. Hence the threat of scourging and the centurion's wise word of caution. Paul was now in the hands of the Romans. He was to remain there for five years.

Now for the fifth time the supreme court of Jewry was to adjudicate on the claims of the Christian Church. Lysias obviously had full briefing on how to deal with the Jewish leaders. Rome was handling the situation of deepening menace in her most turbulent province with care. Eager to fulfil all the requirements of justice, and in pursuance of an enlightened policy towards the Jews which Pilate's heavy-handed attitude towards that difficult people had more than ever shown to be necessary, Lysias set Paul before the senior tribunal of his own people, and found it necessary in the outcome (10) to rescue the prisoner a second time.

Paul's dexterous conduct must have astonished him. The atrocious action of the high priest, in such contrast to the disciplined attitude of the Romans, enraged Paul. How it was that he failed to recognize the high priest is a matter of conjecture. He had, of course, been long absent from Jerusalem, and if his swift reaction contrasted with that of Christ on a like occasion, it conformed to common norms of human conduct which most people will too readily recognize.

Paul could see that constructive argument would be fruitless, and appealed to his own class, the Pharisees, with whom he at least had a point of contact. The worldly, venal, heretical Sadducees were in any case beyond all argument of piety or reason.

F. W. Farrar, one of Paul's early great biographers, condemns Paul for thus dividing the assembly, but Ramsay has a convincing reply. 'His defence was always the same,' says Ramsay, 'and therefore carefully planned: that his life had been consistently directed towards one end, the glorification of the God of Israel by admitting the Nations to be His servants, and that this was true Judaism and true Pharisaism.' Hence the relevance of the defence before the Sanhedrin. 'If one party,' Ramsay continues, 'was more capable of being brought to a favourable view of his claims than the other he would naturally and justifiably aim at affecting the minds of the more hopeful party.' That is exactly what Paul did at Athens, when he addressed himself almost exclusively to the Stoic element in his audience. He was claiming, moreover, 'to represent the true line of development in which Judaism ought to advance'.

34: Paul and the Plotters

Acts 23.11–15; 2 Corinthians 11.16–33

We might pause a moment to try to imagine Paul's state of mind. He had just passed through days of terrible mental and spiritual stress. He had escaped a plot against his life, and was about to hear of another. He had been twice rescued by force from the insane violence of his own people. He must have been deeply hurt by the narrow-minded group of his own fellow Christians who had demanded a demonstration of formal agreement with their erroneous prejudices, and in so doing had opened the path to catastrophe.

He must also have been overwhelmed by misgivings, for he had battled his way to Jerusalem and disastrous suffering against road-block after road-block of advice to retreat. Like Abraham, who had flung his hastily armed shepherds against an invading force from the Euphrates Valley, and had faced, in the outcome, and with time to weigh the consequences, a painful collapse of confidence (Gen. 14), Paul needed a word from God (11). The great Abraham was his hero. He had pondered deeply over the life and adventures of the patriarch. It seems not by accident that, in his moment of crisis, in those sombre hours of the night when the darkness of heaven seems to penetrate the soul, he received a word from the Lord which is almost an echo of the word which came to Abraham (Gen. 15.1).

51

The encouragement sets no seal of divine approval on Paul's journey to Jerusalem. The wisdom of that enterprise still stands open to question. But it is like God in such dark hours of the soul to show some token of His love. And there came in confirmation the revelation of the plot by the forty Jews. It was a climax of hate. There is, unfortunately, no evidence that the plotters, frustrated of their purpose, starved to death by the terms of their vow. The scribes and lawyers had sophistic devices by which they could circumvent any of the inconveniences with which they had loaded the Mosaic law, and it is quite certain that there were hypocritical escape clauses whereby the plotters could extricate themselves from the ultimate consequences of the hunger and thirst they had undertaken to face. It is a not uncommon situation in life that a revelation of God's care should stand in juxtaposition to a demonstration of human viciousness.

35: Paul's Nephew

Acts 23.16–35

The plot, quite unexpectedly, throws a ray of light on Paul's family, the only scrap of information we possess. If the secret plotting of the fanatics became known to Paul's sister, the family must have had the highest connections in the city. It was, moreover, an act of no small courage thus to lay information. The deference with which Lysias treats the boy is also notable.

Loyalty is a pleasant sight, and after his night of darkness, Paul must have seen in his sister's and his nephew's love yet another token of God's continuing care for him. And it would come with greater sweetness to him if such loyalty was seen against the background of family repudiation. John Pollock, commenting on Paul's home circumstances, remarks: 'My personal reading of the scanty extant evidence is that Paul was ... a widower, or, more probably, had been repudiated by his wife when he returned to Tarsus a Christian—he suffered the loss of all things for Christ.'

However this may be, Paul's sister and her son saved Paul's life. The efficient Lysias set arrangements in train. It is a deeply significant fact that it required a detachment of 470 troops to ensure the safety of one political prisoner travelling down the descending highway to Caesarea—probably the high road down to the coastal plain where the shattered trucks and jeeps lie in the scrub as a memorial of another guerrilla-haunted day. The situation in Palestine must have been grave indeed, and it seems clear that firm Roman control was practically confined to the cities.

The chapter closes with a last glance at the tribune. He takes a small liberty with truth when he advances the hour of his regard for Paul's status as a Roman. It was a neater story, set Lysias in a somewhat more favourable light, and is quite in character. He was a good type of officer, and reinforces the suggestion already made that the imperial government set some store by the type of man chosen for service in Palestine.

Paul was now safe. The garrison port of Caesarea, Rome's bridgehead and stronghold, was completely secure. There was a church community there. Paul was free to write, Luke to pursue his researches through the land. The extensive ruins visible today are of immense Christian significance.

Questions and themes for study and discussion on Studies 28–35

1. Paul and Philip's daughters.
2. Give examples from the Old Testament of symbolic teaching.
3. Is compromise ever justified?
4. Are crowds dangerous? Why and when?
5. The nature of true courage.
6. Pharisaism, good and bad.
7. The nature of hatred.
8. How did Paul spend his time at Caesarea?

THE MISSION OF THE CHURCH

Mission and the Holy Spirit

36: Empowering for Mission

John 15.22–16.11; 20.19–23

The word 'Comforter' (**15**.26, AV [KJV]), used to translate the Greek word *paraklētos*, can be traced back to Wycliff, when the word then denoted the giving of strength and courage (cf. Latin *fortis* meaning 'brave'). 400 years have passed and the verb 'to comfort' has mellowed with the years! Jesus spoke to His disciples primarily of an Enabler, an empowering Companion (cf. Eph. **3**.16). He would also be the 'Spirit of truth' (**15**.26) whose ministry of witness to Christ would be closely linked with the disciples' own witness to their Master (**15**.27). 'The double witness in the world nevertheless would be one witness . . . the witness of the Spirit and the witness of the Church' (Leon Morris). The Spirit witnesses because He is 'the Spirit of Christ' (Rom. **8**.9; 1 Pet. **1**.11), glorifying Christ (**16**.14). The disciples witness because their eyes have seen and their hands have touched (1 John **1**.1 ff.), and they are thus inescapably and joyously committed.

All true power in mission is to be found in the working of the Spirit in the hearts of men (**16**.8). In respect of any awareness of truth, 'whatever conscience the world might display is His work' (Donald Guthrie). Through Him, men will realize the tragedy of rejecting Jesus for self-centred independency (**16**.9); they will acknowledge the genuineness and rightness of all that Jesus claimed to be because of His triumphant vindication from this earthly scene (**16**.10), and they will tremble with guilt as they see the cause of evil, to which they have given allegiance, humbled and broken through Christ's victory (**16**.11). When we begin to appropriate for ourselves the ability to bring about such conviction in men through self-devised means, we are immediately launched on something other than Christian mission. Let personal and mass evangelists beware!

Christ had thus spoken of 'the coming One'; now He appoints His disciples for service in the Spirit's power (20.21 f.). In our Lord's use of two different words to mean 'send' in v. 21, Jesus is in fact saying: 'As the Father has commissioned me by delegating to me His authority, so I now despatch you under that same authority.' And to knit the disciples' mission with the promised Holy Spirit, He 'blows' or breathes on them probably in symbolic anticipation of the day when the Spirit would truly 'blow' on them (cf. Acts 2.2 ff.) and they would fully 'receive' Him (cf. Acts 2.38; 10.47). Such empowering is necessary if God's Word is to be convincingly declared to men regarding their sins (cf. 20.23). The Church can but declare what God has already done (cf. Mark 2.7; 1 John 1.9), and while human knowledge can never be omniscient, yet the Christian can confidently declare to the one who truly repents and believes: 'Your sins have been forgiven for His sake' (1 John 2.12, NEB).

How much of the Spirit's 'convicting' work have you seen among your friends in recent days?

37: Categories of Salvation

Luke 24.44–53

The average Jew read about the Messiah in his Old Testament with his eyes open but his mind closed. 'It cannot be that the Messiah will suffer and die; when He comes, it will be as an all-triumphant King!' he wistfully trusted. So a task of 'thoroughly opening up' (the literal meaning of the Greek verb *dianoigō*) was needed (45) for those 'startled and frightened' disciples (37). Jesus showed that not only His suffering, death and resurrection (46) but also the proclaiming of salvation world-wide were foreshadowed in the pages of the sacred book. 'The picture, blurred, indistinct, out of focus, came sharply into focus and they saw the whole thing not in detail but in sequence' (Campbell Morgan).

Never would such tidings as this sound on men's ears! Here were spiritual categories after which men had groped and grasped from the earliest dawn of time and have similarly sought to the present day. The message is centred in two truths. The first is repentance, *metanoia*, that turning from self to God as a result of a humbling awareness of having offended and rebelled against

55

Him in thought, word and deed. It is a recurrent theme in the Old Testament as God called His people to turn to Him from their waywardness (Isa. 55.7; Jer. 3.12 f, etc.). The need for men to repent was prominent in the message of Jesus (Matt. 4.17, etc.) and in that of the Early Church too (Acts 2.38, etc.). The second category of God's saving message is forgiveness of sins, *aphesis hamartiōn*, that act of God whereby He ceases to reckon a man's misdeeds against him and accounts him guiltless before His bar of justice. Again, it emerges prominently in the Old Testament (Psa. 103.3; Dan. 9.9, etc.), in the teaching of Jesus (Matt. 6.12, etc.) and in the witness of the first Christians (Acts 5.31, etc.). In the saving purposes of God, repentance in fact 'brings' forgiveness (47), and these two are only to be found 'in Christ's Name'. It is for this reason that the gospel stands unique by comparison with the world's secular ideologies and religious teachings.

The proclamation of these tidings had to begin at Jerusalem (47) because it was the historical and symbolical centre of God's dealings with His people and thus, in the sovereign purposes of God, the place where they would be 'invested' (A. B. Bruce) with the needful empowering for their task (49). The Father had promised the Spirit through the prophets (cf. Isa. 44.3; Joel 2.28–32). Through His Son (cf. John 7.38 f.) He had now announced His immediate advent (cf. John 14.16, 26. The Greek verb *exapostellō*, I send forth, v. 49, is in the present tense indicating an imminent future action). The disciples' obedience (52) was to be duly rewarded (cf. Acts 5.32).

Is there any salvation for sincere followers of non-Christian religions apart from a conscious experience of repentance and forgiveness 'in His Name' (47)?

38: Enduement for Service

Acts 1.1–11

Jesus lived and taught in the Holy Spirit's power (2, cf. Luke 4.1, 14). Through the same Spirit He both offered up His life in death (Heb. 9.14) and was openly vindicated as the Son of God through resurrection (Rom. 1.4; 1 Tim. 3.16). His promise to the disciples (4) was thus in full accord with the pattern of His own ministry.

John the Baptist had already contrasted his own baptizing in water with the forthcoming baptism in the Holy Spirit to be effected by Jesus (Mark **1**.8; Luke **3**.16). Our Lord restates the contrast with His own unique authority and at a new vantage point in time, full of immediate expectation (5, 'within the next few days' NEB). The verb 'to baptize' means, when used literally, 'to wash by dipping or immersing' or when used figuratively 'to overwhelm, to plunge into a new realm of experience'. It was in this latter figurative sense that Jesus used the word in relation to the disciples' impending encounter with the Holy Spirit, in the same way that He used the verb 'to clothe' in Luke **24**.49. The terminology of 'baptism' was especially significant in view of the later reference to the Spirit being 'poured out' (**2**.17, 18, 33; **10**.45); the disciples were to be submerged in the Spirit's tidal flow as the New Age was inaugurated. We must be aware of the danger of allowing these and other figurative expressions found in the New Testament relating to the work of the Holy Spirit in the believer's life to harden into 'technical terms', so that a Christian's spiritual standing is measured by how many of them apply to him.

The 'coming upon' them of the Spirit (note the further graphic phrase) would mean power (Gk. *dunamis*, meaning 'ability and strength to perform' as differentiated from *exousia* (7) meaning 'liberty and authority to exercise power', Abbot-Smith). This power would be the motivation for the ministry of witness to which they had been called (8, cf. John **15**.27).

Only the Spirit can enable the Church to reach the geographical limits of its task; for not only Jerusalem and its immediate environs would need to hear the good news, but also the whole province of Judea, the neighbouring northern 'half-caste' territory of Samaria and then 'lands without limit' (8).

*We can grieve and quench the Holy Spirit (Eph. **4**.30; 1 Thess. **5**.19) in mission as well as in other aspects of Christian living.*

39: Experience of Promise

Acts 2

'At Pentecost, the Holy Spirit empowered a little band of insignificant, ignorant and feeble but believing men and women to undertake the stupendous task of conquering the world for

Christ, their Lord' (R. B. Kuiper). Pentecost (1, meaning 'the fiftieth') fell 50 days after the presentation of the wave sheaf at Passover (cf. Lev. 23.15–21; Deut. 16.9–12). It was one of the three great Jewish festivals to which every Jew, resident within 20 miles of Jerusalem, was bound to come. According to Edersheim, it probably attracted more visitors from a distance than even the Passover itself.

The supernatural and external signs of 'driving wind' and 'flames of fire' (2 f., NEB) were those frequently linked with the power and presence of God (cf. Psa. 104.4; Exod. 19.18). They symbolized an inward experience, the 'filling' of the disciples with the Holy Spirit. That which was promised (1.5, cf. John 15.26) came to pass. We should understand this yet further figurative verb 'to fill' not in the static sense of 'to top-up an empty vessel' but in the dynamic sense of 'to take possession of' or 'control' (cf. 3.10; 5.3, 17; 19.29).

As the Holy Spirit began to fulfil His ministry of interpreting spiritual truth through the disciples (cf. John 15.26). the international crowd, gathered in Jerusalem (9 ff.), began to hear 'the great things God has done' (11, NEB). This came firstly through a miraculously given communication in their own individual dialects (8), and then in straightforward *koinē* Greek or Aramaic (14 ff.; it is not certain which language Peter used here.)

The main purpose of the pouring out of the Spirit (cf. 17 ff.; Joel 2.28–32) was to inaugurate an era when men could call on the name of the Lord and be saved (21). Peter's own clear and illumined presentation of the gospel (22 ff.) was yet a further illustration of this same Spirit of truth at work (John 16.13 f.), for Peter could never have grasped such truths about the Old Testament or his Lord on his own (cf. Matt. 16.17)!

The availability of the Holy Spirit to the obedient and believing is proclaimed by the disciples in their turn to the enquiring crowds (38), and thus it has been passed on in successive ages to people 'far away' (39, NEB).

When did you last 'pass on' the offer?

58

40: Crossing of Boundaries

Acts 8

The unleashing of persecution against the early believers (1) only served to widen the extent of their witness (4) and Philip moves into Samaritan territory to make Christ known there to mighty effect (5 ff., cf. John 4.4 ff.). Unless we are to accuse Philip of preaching a truncated gospel, which would not appear evident from vs. 5, 35, 40, and to assume the response of the Samaritans to have been spurious, which would not seem to be the natural interpretation of vs. 6, 8, 14, those baptized were truly born again of God's Spirit (cf. John 3.5), had received the Spirit (cf. Gal. 3.2) and were thus indwelt by Him (cf. Rom. 8.9–11; 1 Cor. 3.16). We must thus interpret the verb 'receive' in vs. 17, 19 in terms of the parallel and further figurative verb 'fall on' in v. 16, the latter being used on other occasions when the 'reception' of the Spirit was accompanied by speaking in tongues and similar manifestations (cf. 10.44, 46; 11.15, cf. 19.6 where another pictorial verb 'came upon' is used). 'In the case of the Samaritans no such signs from heaven had followed their baptism, and the Apostles prayed for a conspicuous divine sanction on the reception of the new converts' (A. B. Bruce). It is logical to conclude that what Simon 'saw' (18) and what he thought he could reproduce himself (19) was 'a Samaritan Pentecost', and the laying on of hands (17) was the outward expression of that inner bond of spiritual unity (cf. Eph. 4.3) which Jerusalem and Samaritan believers now enjoyed through their common faith in Christ.

The Spirit of God then directed Philip to minister in a much more individualized situation (26, cf. v. 29). The Ethiopian court official's visit to Jerusalem was prompted by his desire to worship God (27) in contrast to the primitive cultic deities venerated by his fellow-countrymen. 'His conversion (36 ff.) marks a further advance towards the evangelization of the Gentiles' (F. F. Bruce). The joy with which he continued on his way was surely as much a product of the Spirit's working (Gal. 5.22) as were Philip's new directives for service (39, cf. 1 Kings 18.12; 2 Kings 2.16).

How sensitive are you to the promptings of the Spirit for mission in your life (29) and how eager are you to obey (30)?

41: Fulfilling of Prophecy

Acts 10

The great moment had come! Peter had already shared in the taking of the gospel to semi-Gentiles (**8.**14 ff.). Now God was to use him to make the major break-through to the wholly Gentile world. As with other passages of Scripture, while the Spirit is only specifically mentioned on selected occasions (19 f., 38, 44 f., 47) the evidence of His activity is to be seen throughout the narrative, which because of its importance is recorded in the next chapter when recounted by Peter himself (**11.**1–18).

Despite the godliness of Cornelius and his household (2), he was still traditionally regarded as 'unclean' by such as Peter, for in Jewish eyes, Gentile carelessness with food made social intercourse with them out of the question. God showed Peter (9 ff.) that the areas where He is at work must never be treated with disdain (15) and such an area was this Gentile household (22). With his spiritual understanding clearing at every move (21, 23, 25), Peter confessed how the Spirit of God was changing his traditional prejudices (28). In response to Cornelius' invitation (33) he pointed his hearers to Christ and His power to forgive 'everyone who believes in Him' (43). This inclusive 'everyone' was a consequence of Peter's recognition that God has no favourites (34) and that He is ready to accept the sincere seekings of any person by bringing to them, through His messengers, the news of salvation. We note that Cornelius was not saved on the grounds of his religious sincerity (2, 35) but by his personal trust in Christ (47, cf. **11.**17 f.). It is mistaken to conclude from this passage, therefore, that 'religious sincerity' is sufficient to save.

This time, the Holy Spirit 'fell' (44, cf. **8.**16) and was 'poured out' (45, cf. **2.**17 f., 33) before those who had received Him had been baptized in water (47 f.). 'No routine procedure would have availed for so unprecedented a situation as the acceptance of the gospel by Gentiles; an unmediated act of God was required' writes F. F. Bruce. The unfolding purposes of God in the Old Testament had broken forth in wonder and grace; Jew and Gentile had become 'fellow citizens ... of the household of God', 'members of the same body', 'all one in Christ Jesus' (Eph. **2.**19; **3.**6; Gal. **3.**28). Peter was convinced that God's dealings with both were now without distinction (cf. **11.**15, 17 f.) and from the

60

ruins of Jewish traditionalism there was rising the new building of the Church of Jesus Christ.

Can you see any 'traditional structures' in missionary activity today that need renewing by the Holy Spirit?

42: Establishing of Principles

Romans 15.7–21

Paul delights to present Christ as the inaugurator of God's blessings to both Jew and Gentile (8 f.) and draws from the rich veins of the Law, the Prophets and the Writings (the 3 great divisions of the Old Testament) to illustrate the Gentile inheritance in particular (9–12). Isaiah's note of 'hope' (12, cf. Isa. 11.10) makes a suitable launching pad for him to glorify the God who through His Spirit can make the believer 'overflow with hope' (13, NEB) in the surging confidence that what God has promised will assuredly come true (cf. 5.4; 15.4; Col. 1.27).

Turning to his personal pattern of service 'to the Gentiles' (16), he uses Jewish sacerdotal terminology to describe himself as a priest (Gk. *leitourgos*), his ministry as 'priestly service' (Gk. *hierourgōn*) and the Gentiles as the priestly offering (Gk. *prosphora*) that he presents (16). Perhaps having in mind Jewish believers who might quibble at the correctness of such an 'unclean' offering, Paul declares it 'acceptable' by the operations of the Holy Spirit. Through that Spirit men's hearts are cleansed by faith (cf. Acts 15.8 f.) and in Him 'the true circumcision', comprising both Jew and Gentile, worship God and find joy in Jesus Christ (Phil. 3.3).

Despite the high privilege of being called to minister in such a 'priestly service' Paul's only glory continues to be in Christ. His finished work at Calvary (Gal. 6.14) and continuing work through His servants (18) in the power of the Spirit (19) dominate Paul's heart and mind. Only endued with the Spirit's power could he have demonstrated the divine origin of the gospel through miraculous signs (cf. Acts 19.11) and preached its truth in every major area of the Roman provinces bordering the Eastern Mediterranean (19 f.). Truly, 'the Holy Spirit is a missionary Spirit creating in God's servants an internal necessity to preach the gospel' (Roland Allen).

'Activity world-wide in its direction and intention . . . is inevitable for us unless we are ready to deny the Holy Spirit of Christ' (*Roland Allen*).

Questions and themes for study and discussion on Studies 36–42

1. 'It is in the revelation of the Holy Spirit as a missionary Spirit that the Acts stands alone in the New Testament.' How far is Roland Allen justified in this statement?
2. How can Christians hinder the Spirit's ministry in world missions today?
3. In what ways can the 'figurative' verbs relating to the Holy Spirit's coming to the Early Church be applied to the Church today?

CHARACTER STUDIES

*43: Felix

Acts 23.26; 24.1–10, 22–27

Felix, like Pilate, was a lamentable mistake. All sorts of ir-
regularities disgraced his governorship. He was the brother of
Pallas, the notorious freedman and senior minister of Claudius,
an upstart of whom Tacitus, the mordant Roman historian,
speaks with blistering scorn. He is no less contemptuous of Felix
who, he said, 'thought he could commit every sort of iniquity
and escape the consequences.' He felt secure under his powerful
brother's shadow. Nothing could be more untrue than the
opening gambit of Tertullus' artificial oratory. We have seen
what state the country was in from the fact that Lysias detached
the major part of a cohort to secure the safe arrival of Paul in
Caesarea.

Such was the man before whom Paul preached of 'righteousness, self-control, and judgement' and who put off consideration
of such things until a 'more convenient season'. Tacitus mentions him again in describing the events which led up to the
rebellion. He describes him as 'a master of cruelty and lust who
exercised the powers of a king in the spirit of a slave'. Nero recalled him in A.D. 56 or 57, and he passes from the scene.

The scene in court is dramatic, a striking illustration of the
lines of James Russell Lowell:

Truth forever on the scaffold, Wrong forever on the throne,
Yet that scaffold sways the future, and, behind the dim unknown,
Standeth God within the shadow, keeping watch above His own.

For a brief moment Felix seemed to have been touched with
fear, and faced himself. He is visibly confronted with a crisis and
makes a decision. His greed was the last factor which turned the
scales. There is no 'more convenient season' than the passing
moment when the vital choices of life are to be made. As Lowell's
same poem puts it:

Once to every man and nation comes the moment to decide,
In the strife of Truth with Falsehood, for the good or evil side . . .

Felix was tangled, like his predecessor Pilate, in a web of his own weaving. As with Pilate, it would have taken a mighty act of the will to rise and cut himself free. He was unable to make that painful reappraisement and died as he lived.

*44: Drusilla

Acts 24.24

Drusa (Drusilla is a pet-name as Priscilla is of Prisca) was one of the daughters of Agrippa I. She married, probably about A.D. 53, Azis of Emesa, a principality in the north of Syria. In the following year, still only about sixteen years of age, she was seduced by Felix, and became that scoundrel's third wife, a situation which provoked contempt even in Rome. It was probably the influence of Drusilla's sister, Bernice, and Agrippa II, after Claudius' death and the consequent passing of Felix' protection, that secured the recall of Felix from his mismanaged governorship.

According to Josephus, who, as Vespasian's secretary, and a Jewish historian, is likely to have been in possession of factual knowledge, Drusilla bore Felix a son, whom she named Agrippa, after her father. She survived her husband's recall, and subsequent death, and lived in the Campanian town of Pompeii until August A.D. 79. On the 24th of that month, Vesuvius exploded in the famous eruption which Pliny describes vividly in two letters to his friend the historian Tacitus. Drusilla and her son appear to have perished under the ash which sealed Pompeii for the discoveries of the modern world. Some Jewish slave wrote 'Sodoma Gomora' on a wall, possibly when doom descended. Could it have been Drusilla's house? She was 39 or 40 years of age.

Drusilla must have had some knowledge of her father's unfortunate relations with the Christians. She had the immense privilege of hearing a direct appeal from the most famous Christian of her day. She heard Paul preach of 'righteousness, self-control and judgement to come.' It is intriguing to imagine what she may have remembered of words in that distant courtroom, when the great mushroom cloud 'like a pine tree', said Pliny, referring to the umbrella pines of his land, rose above the shaking land on that hot August day, and the mephitic vapours began to roll, under dense darkness, on the little city.

Like Felix, whose importunity had seemed to open such vast

possibilities of romance, excitement, social standing, and travel overseas, she too came to the end of the road. It is the end which counts in the affairs of life. She chose disastrously, had the chance to choose aright, and lost her opportunity.

45: Tertullus

Acts 24.1–9; James 3.1–10

Before leaving the scene in the Caesarea court, it may be interesting to look briefly at the orator Tertullus. He was possibly a Roman trained in the principles of rhetoric fashionable in the capital. Roman oratory, deprived of its political themes with the establishment of the imperial autocracy, flourished in the schools and the courts. Soon after Paul's death, Quintilian returned from Spain to Rome, and his work on rhetoric is one of the few surviving pieces of Latin literature from that century.

The study of the principles of speech and of persuasion can be mentally and morally damaging. Debate for the sake of debate can weaken regard for truth, and it is the duty of any speaker and any hearer to consider content and truth before the manner and method of its presentation. Aristophanes, the great Athenian writer of satirical comedy, attacking the New Education in his play *The Clouds*, quips that the object of sophistic instruction in his day was 'to make the worse appear the better reason'. Tertullus was of such a class.

Tertullus, in fact, was no great orator. Felix, scoundrel though he was, seems to have been quite unimpressed by the suggestion that a case of treason was on his hands. The prosecution made a serious mistake in directing a side-blow against the capable commander of the Jerusalem garrison. Felix knew that his covertly corrupt rule depended on the efficiency of such officers. Nor, in fact, was the plausible fellow well-trained in his corrupt art. In oratory the greatest art is to conceal art, and Luke seems to take a subtle pleasure in reporting the prosecutor's too obviously elaborate flatteries, an obsequious approach no doubt somewhat dimmed by the sour presence of the high priest in the court.

Commenting on such rhetoric, the cynical Lord Chesterfield said: 'Elegance of style and the turn of the periods, make the chief impression upon the hearers. Most people have ears, but few have judgement. Tickle those ears, and, depend upon it, you will

catch their judgement, such as it is.' Misreading Felix, the San-
hedrists thought to apply such advice. They failed, probably
because of Felix' regard for Lysias, whose further advice he
thought it prudent to await. It is fairly obvious that, when the
tribune came to Caesarea, he counselled prudence. It is to be
hoped that Tertullus was not paid his fee. The world has had
enough of those who use words to hide the truth.

46: Festus

Acts 25.1–27; 26.24, 25

Porcius Festus succeeded to the mismanaged procuratorship in
A.D. 57 or 58, and the brief episode of his examination of Paul and
the consultation with Agrippa II is another interesting glimpse of
a Roman governor at work in a difficult situation. Festus had
inherited from Felix a lamentable load of trouble. There was
lawlessness in the countryside, and armed rivalry between the
factions of the hierarchy. Events were in full flow for the disaster
of eight years later. Festus could not afford to alienate collaborating elements, and the determination of the priests to make away
with an obviously innocent man was a problem which required
most careful handling. It was the situation of thirty years before,
repeated with other actors and on another stage. Festus, however, was a luckier man than Pilate. He found a way of escape
through the prisoner's own action. He had offered Paul an
acquittal on the charge of sedition, and added the proposal, not
unreasonable from his point of view, that the ex-Pharisee should
face a religious investigation before his peers.

For Paul it was a crisis. He knew the perils of Jerusalem.
Perhaps he grasped the realities of the political situation, the
growing tension, and the deepening anarchy, better than the
procurator himself. If Festus found himself inhibited by official
policy from refusing and frustrating the Jerusalem hierarchy,
Paul proposed to cut the knot, to save himself and free the governor from all embarrassment by exercising a Roman citizen's
right. He appealed to Caesar.

The process to which Paul had recourse was the act by which a
litigant disputes a judgement, with the consequence that the case
is referred to a higher court, normally that of the authority who
had originally appointed the magistrate of the court from which

the appeal originated. Caesar had appointed Festus. Festus was obliged to accept the appeal, and refer it on, accompanied by relevant documents and a personal report, which must have presented some difficulty. He saw no fault in Paul by any standards of law and justice familiar to him. He was newly arrived in Palestine, and Jewish law and Jewish religion were both unfamiliar to him. In his difficult office he was not free to sweep such matters aside with a Gallio's contempt. Festus had his career to make. His difficult province was a hard testing-ground, and the lucidity and correct terminology of a document over his signature in a court so exalted as that of Caesar himself must have been a matter of anxious concern. Hence the alacrity with which he availed himself of the help of Agrippa II.

The Jews had no complaints to level against Festus. He was possibly the best of the procurators. It is a pity that he died two years or thereabouts later.

47: Agrippa II

Acts 25.13–27; 26.1–3, 25–32

Agrippa was a man of ability, of wide knowledge of Judaism, and of more than a nodding acquaintance with Christianity. He must have known the policy of his house. Paul's attitude and careful apologia show that he valued the opportunity, doubtless for the sake of the Church and its freedom, equally with his own. It was of prime importance to the prisoner, as well as to the procurator, that the report to Rome should be accurately phrased and properly supplied with detail. It is an interesting situation. The careful governor, obviously anxious not to make a false step amid the growing perils of the province; the care of Rome's representative to honour the client-king, so true to official policy as old as Augustus; Paul's battle for justice, so often to be repeated; the background of menace outside the safety of the garrison town—where else in ancient literature is so authentic a document of the Empire in action to be found?

There is little more to say of Herod's house. Agrippa makes one or two brief appearances in later history. Josephus shows him actively and despairingly at work in an endeavour to preserve the peace in Palestine, when the great rebellion was looming. With the sure diplomatic instinct of his family, he was active in support of Vespasian, the successful survivor of the troubled year of civil war which followed Nero's death. He was actually in Rome, whither Vespasian had sent him, to salute Galba, the first of that year's ill-fated emperors. In Tacitus' brief phrases it is possible to catch a glimpse of the old decision and sure choice characteristic of others of his house: 'Soon after, Agrippa, informed by private message from the East, left Rome before Vitellius received the news, and hurried back on a fast ship. With equal spirit Queen Berenice espoused Vespasian's cause. She was in the bloom of her youth and beauty, and had made herself agreeable to Vespasian, old though he was, by the magnificence of her gifts.' It was not the first bold voyage of a Herod across the sea between Italy and Palestine. Agrippa took an active part in the war in Palestine, was wounded at Gamala, and was with Titus at the siege of Jerusalem. From the safety of Caesarea he saw the final ruin of the country he had sought to save. With Agrippa II ended the Herods, an astonishingly able family, whose pro-Roman policy went far to postpone the clash between Rome and the Jews, and played in consequence an unwitting but significant part in holding the peace during the formative years of the Christian Church in Palestine.

Josephus, who, as archaeology proceeds, proves a more and more reliable guide, is the supplier of most of the information on the king.

48: Bernice (Berenice)

Acts 25.13–27

We have looked at this passage before in connection with Agrippa the Second, but the remarkable woman who accompanied the king is also worth consideration. She was a daughter of Agrippa the First, sister to Agrippa the Second and Drusilla, and was born in A.D. 28. Her first husband was one Marcus, a Jewish official of Alexandria who soon died. Herod Agrippa the First then betrothed her to her uncle, also a Herod by name, the ruler, under Claudius, of the kingdom of Calchis. Of this marriage there were two sons. Herod of Calchis died in A.D. 48.

As a widow Bernice lived in close friendship with her brother, and there seems to have been a strong bond between them—with the inevitable result that rumours of an incestuous relationship were rife. Even in distant Rome, half a century later, the rumour was still remembered, and Juvenal wrote in his Sixth Satire, sometimes called 'The Legend of Bad Women' of

> *That far-famed gem which Berenice wore,*
> *The hire of incest and thence valued more,*
> *A brother's present, in that barbarous state*
> *Where kings the sabbath barefoot celebrate,*
> *And old indulgence grants a length of life*
> *To hogs that fatten fearless of the knife.*

Of this allegation there is no concrete evidence whatsoever, nor of the actual marriage of brother and sister—an arrangement not uncommon in the East.

Bernice was present in Jerusalem when the procurator Florus pillaged the Temple in those last tragic acts of Roman folly which preceded the outbreak of revolt. She risked her life in begging him to show sense and desist, and was almost killed by Florus' undisciplined troops. She wrote to the proconsul Cestius in Syria to complain of Florus, and stood, in superb courage, by her brother's side, when he appealed to the Jerusalem crowd to abstain from violence. The mob burned the palaces of both brother and sister when rebellion broke out. The couple took refuge in Caesarea.

For all this information, which sets the brother and sister in a rather fine light, we are indebted to Josephus. Tacitus, the Roman historian, picks up the story at this point, and he tells how Agrippa and Bernice swore allegiance to Vespasian. According to Suetonius, Bernice and Titus, Vespasian's son and short lived successor, were lovers, and only such prejudice as still lived in Juvenal who was quoted above, prevented Titus from marrying her. Hers was a strange and lurid career. At Caesarea she too had her hour of opportunity.

Questions and themes for study and discussion on Studies 43–48

1. Paul's text before Felix. What times are 'convenient' for decision?
2. Drusilla's fault and folly.

3. The use and abuse of oratory.
4. Appealing to Caesar.
5. 'Almost you persuade me . . .'
6. 'The hour of opportunity.'

THE MISSION OF THE CHURCH

Mission and the Church

49: Men Needed

Luke 9.1–6; 10.1–20

To keep company with Christ involves personal commitment to His purposes. For the twelve disciples, this meant being available for mission. Notice the verbal sequence: 'He called the twelve (1) . . . He gave them power (1) . . . He sent them out (2)' (cf. Mark 3.14 f.). This embodies a spiritual succession that is apparent throughout Scripture, from God's dealings with Moses (Exod. 3.4, 10 f.) and the prophets (Jer. 1.5–9) to His commissioning of the Early Church (Luke 24.48 f.) and of Paul (Acts 26.16 ff.). The verb *apostellō* translated 'to send' (2) is the root from which the word 'apostle' is derived and basically means 'to send out with instructions to act on the authority of the sender and in his name'. It was in this capacity, then, that the twelve moved out among the towns and villages of Trans-Jordania (6).

The 'heralding' for which they had been appointed was a triumphant announcement that God's kingly rule had begun on earth (2), and this was to be demonstrated not only in word but also in the practical overthrow of Satan's power over men (1, 6, cf. 10.17). If the twelve were sent primarily to minister in this way among the Jews (cf. Matt. 10.5 f. the total probably symbolizing the number of the tribes of Israel), the commissioning of the seventy (10.1, or 'seventy-two' as indicated by a good number of Greek mss. cf. NEB and TEV) could well have had a wider ministry in view (the number is reminiscent of the total of the Gentile nations in Gen. 10 or of the eldership of Israel [Exod. 24.1]). Yet, encouraging as were these wider circles of ministry, they could only touch part of the need, and in the light of the immensity of the task before them, Jesus again urges His disciples to prayer (cf. Matt. 9.37 f., John 4.35), making 'the seventy' the first part of the answer (10.3)!

With what readiness to become personally involved do you sing the words: 'Send forth the Gospel, let it run southwards and northwards, east and west'?

50: Men Transformed

Matthew 16.13–28

The conviction to which Peter came concerning the person of Christ (16) was both forthright and divinely inspired (17, cf. 1 Cor. **12**.3), and the expressing of it led to our Lord enunciating a major truth regarding His redeeming purposes among men. The confession of Himself as Christ and Son of God (16) or, alternatively, the actual person confessing this truth (both are possible interpretations of v. 18) would be the material upon which He would build the spiritual edifice He called 'His Church'.

The word *ekklesia*, translated 'church', literally means 'that which is called out', and was a word widely used in our Lord's day. In the Graeco-Roman world, it had come to describe any local assembly of Roman citizens, whether democratically convened for legislative purposes or gathered for more informal purposes. In the Greek version of the Old Testament, it is used over seventy times to denote an assembly of the people of Israel summoned to hear what God had to say to them (cf. Deut. **18**.16). The suitability of such a word to denote the new community that Jesus would be bringing into being through the gospel is clearly evident, and it became one of the great words of the New Testament. It denoted both the local fellowship of believers (e.g. 1 Cor. **1**.2; 1 Thess. **1**.1), as well as that wider, all-inclusive fellowship of which the individual fellowship was a local expression (e.g. Acts **20**.28; 1 Cor. **10**.32). God's salvation is thus not only to be experienced personally but corporately as well, as believers are joined in fellowship together.

In the Acts, we must therefore see those who responded to the gospel in such places as Jerusalem, Antioch and the cities of Galatia in terms of Christ building His Church. Similarly, we note how closely Paul's ministry was bound up with the planting and nourishing of local churches in every place he visited. All true mission today should have the same end in view.

Because the Church of Jesus Christ is made up of those in whose lives the power of Satan has been overthrown (cf. the previous study; also Acts **26**.18; Col. **1**.13), it will never be overpowered by the forces of death (18, NEB). In its outward expression on earth, it may be marred by human deficiencies (e.g. Acts **5**.1–11), suffer setbacks from its enemies (e.g. Acts **12**.1–4) and, as in the case of North Africa in the 7th and China in the 20th centuries, be almost obliterated for a time in certain geographical areas. Yet, because the Church belongs to Christ, the direction and culmination of God's purposes through it are sure (cf. Eph. **5**.22 ff.; Rev. **5**.9 f.).

How far have you realized the personal implications of believing in 'one holy, catholic (i.e. universal) and apostolic church' (Nicene Creed)?

51: Men Invited

Matthew 22.1–14

While numerous critics have considered this parable to be an edited duplicate of that found in Luke **14**.16–24, there is no reason at all why our Lord should not have used the same central theme with variations to serve two connected, though different, purposes. The emphasis in the Lukan parable is on the open graciousness of the inviter; in the Matthaean version, it is on the solemn responsibility of the invitee.

Despite a double call (3 f. at least *one* was customary in the Near East at that time), those summoned treated the invitation with disdain (3, 5). While critics have sought to view vs. 6 f. as a later interpolation in the light of the fall of Jerusalem and with allusion to **21**.35 ff., the textual evidence for this is meagre in the extreme. In any case, if the wedding was to be the occasion for the public recognition of the king's son as the royal heir, such action as described in these two verses would have been justified. The invitation to the wedding went on to be offered to others without regard to status or manner of life (9 f.) and such invitees responded with gratifying readiness and in ample numbers (10). Few Jews hearing the parable could have failed to read the message!

However, responsibility does not end with an outward gesture. An appropriate robe was evidently available on request for all guests attending a feast of such importance. In spite of this, one man showed manifest disregard for the high honour of the occasion (11 f.) 'His conduct argued utter insensibility regarding that to which he had been called' (Edersheim). Previous unpreparedness was no excuse for not availing oneself of that which was both necessary and proper and the penalty for such flagrant haughtiness was exclusion from the inner brilliancy of the banqueting hall into 'outer darkness' (13).

True evangelism involves 'persuasion' as well as 'proclamation', not in the sense of pressurizing people into the Kingdom but by urging upon them, with true compassion, God's gracious offer of salvation (cf. Acts 2.40 f.; 24.25 ff.) Those who reject such an offer, especially through such downright indifference as has been illustrated for us in this parable, will be held responsible for their actions. The lines of divine judgement in Scripture are clearly drawn (13 f., cf. Acts 17.31) and one of the greatest tragedies of the contemporary world is a complete unawareness of their reality.

What are some of the modern parallels of the excuses of v. 5 in relation to men's rejection of the gospel today?

52: Men Challenged

John 21.1–19

A wearying night's fishing (1–3) was transformed by a miracle at daybreak (4–8) and concluded with a lakeside breakfast (9–14). This, in its turn, led on to a personal conversation of moving intimacy between our Lord and Peter (15–19). Since the days when he had been led to Jesus (cf. 1.42), Peter had slowly learned the nature of discipleship, but his brave professions of outstanding loyalty (cf. 13.37; Matt. 26.33) had been shattered by the challenges of a serving maid in the Temple courtyard (cf. Matt. 26.69 ff.). Around the embers of the charcoal fire (9), perhaps withdrawn somewhat from the rest of the disciples, Jesus presses upon Peter the basic realities of spiritual relationship and service.

With the well-known variation in choice of words (see a very helpful discussion of this in W. Hendriksen's commentary on John, pp. 494–500), our Lord probes Peter regarding the comparative nature (15), genuineness (16) and basic quality (17) of his love. To each of Peter's responses, our Lord gives a new commission. Peter, once designated to be 'a fisher of men' (cf. Matt. 4.19) is now called to be a shepherd of men too, and with another gentle movement in the choice of words, Jesus introduces Peter to his ministry of 'providing food for the little ones of the flock' (15), 'caring for the sheep' (16) and 'providing food for the sheep' (17). Jesus had already spoken to His disciples about His own ministry as Shepherd (10.1–30). Now He was disclosing the responsibility of those whom God would appoint to be 'under-shepherds' (cf. Acts 20.28; 1 Pet. 5.2) of His people, that these might be fed 'with knowledge and understanding' (cf. Jer. 3.15).

Among God's gifts to His Church are 'pastors and teachers to equip God's people for work in His service' (Eph. 4.11 f., NEB). The ministry of all such will need Christ's own character and service as their pattern, together with the example of the errant shepherds of Israel in Ezekiel's day (Ezek. 34.1 ff.) serving as a shameful warning against lethargy and irresponsibility.

The Church's mission today needs a more genuine pastoral care both for those within and without its fellowship. It is salutary to be reminded that while this must be expressed particularly by the Church's leaders it should also be evident in the life of each individual Christian (Phil. 2.1 ff.).

Is Christ calling you to 'follow' Him further in a ministry of greater caring for people?

53: Men Commissioned

Matthew 28.16–20; Mark 16.14–20

The whole of our Lord's life was an expression of divine authority (cf. Matt. 11.27; John 3.35; 13.3; 17.2), from His declared prerogative to forgive sins (Matt. 9.6) to His complete control over the disposition of His earthly life (John 10.18). With a retrospective glance at His victory on the Cross (Col. 2.15) and in anticipation of the final culmination of this victory (Phil. 2.9), Jesus again affirms that complete sovereignty is His. This sovereignty had once been subtly but only partially offered to Him by Satan (Matt. 4.8 f.), but which now 'had been given' (aorist tense, indicating a past event) to Him by His Father (Matt. 28.18).

Such universal authority forms the basis of the Church's universal mission (28.19). 'The narrow path within Israel had to branch out into the wide world of all nations' (Karl Barth), and the disciples were commissioned to bring men to be what they themselves already were, administering baptism 'into' or 'as a sign of their new state of belonging to' (Gk. *eis*) the triune God. Discipleship is no less than an entry into a life of loving obedience to Christ (cf. John 14.15) and His presence is pledged to His ambassadors until 'the consummation of the present age' (28.20).

The words of the 'Great Commission' (Matt. 28.18 f.; Mark 16.15) have figured prominently in the motivating reasons for modern missionary movement. At the outset, they were the main source of appeal for William Carey and have been writ large into our missionary literature and hymnology. However, it is important to see them in their wider Biblical context. True missionary motivation can never consist of mere obedience to an external command; it must essentially spring from the energies of the Holy Spirit whose ministry it is to write the law of God on the heart of each believer (cf. Jer. 31.33; John 16.14 f.), moving him in a spontaneous obedience to God's purposes. This is what lay behind Peter's 'we cannot but speak' (Acts 4.20) and all the spontaneous evangelistic zeal so evident in the Early Church.

Note: Mark 16.9–20 was relegated to the margin by the RSV translators but the genuine place of the passage in the apostolic tradition can still be defended, and indeed in the second edition of the RSV it appears in the main body of the text.

How much is an over-emphasis on 'obedience to the Great Commission' as a motive and justification for mission a sign of spiritual decadence within the Church?

54: Men Responsible

1 Corinthians 3.1–23

The cult of personality among the believers at Corinth (4) was evidence both of their spiritual immaturity (2) and carnality (3). Paul 'levels' first himself, the one who first brought the gospel to Corinth (Acts 18.1 ff.), and then Apollos, one of the 'follow up workers' (Acts 18.27 ff.), with a shattering 'what' (5). He moves the spotlight from the 'idolized' Christian worker to the true 'Worker' who deigns to use human instruments so that men may believe (5). Paul and Apollos performed their work of planting and watering but God was the One who continually (for so the Greek tense indicates) caused spiritual life to grow (6). 'The planter and the waterer are nothing compared with Him who gives life to the seed' (7, J. B. Phillips).

The priority of God in the consideration of the Church's task of mission is further emphasized as Paul sees Christians as being 'junior partners' with God in His work, as well as being spheres of God's creative and constructive activity (9). 'When mission has been defined as essentially a human activity or even as man's obedience to God's command, sooner or later its mainspring has snapped under the pressure of events . . . Fundamentally, mission is not man's action but God's; it is for the Christian to choose whether he will be caught up into it and participate in it, or remain outside' (J. V. Taylor).

The precedence of God in mission brings its own solemn responsibility to those who are His instruments. As 'site building supervisors' (10, Gk. *architectōn*) under divine appointment, the manner and materials of their building work must match the nature of the foundation (10 ff.). It may be easier to go for what is cheap and easily available, but there is a time coming when a man's work will be evaluated for what it truly is (13, the word translated 'revealed' means 'shown up in true character'). The New Testament frequently sets this prospect of the final accounting Day of God before us (e.g. 5.5; 2 Cor. 1.14; 2 Pet. 3.12). While a believer's salvation will not be at stake (15, cf. 1 Cor. 9.27) the lasting worthwhileness of his service will be.

How much is your present service truly 'worth' in terms of eternal values?

55: Men Converted

1 Thessalonians 1

The church in the strategically located, Roman provincial capital of Thessalonica (1) had a quality about it that was outstanding. The presentation of the gospel to them in the first instance was not with the customary parade of words expected from travelling orators (cf. 1 Cor. 1.17; 2.4), but with a spiritual power and an exemplary conduct which commended, not contradicted, the message (5, cf. 2.10). The Holy Spirit once again fulfilled the ministry about which Jesus had formerly spoken (John 16.8 ff.) and enabled the Thessalonians to accept the gospel with joy (cf. Gal. 5.22; Rom. 14.17) in the midst of persecution (6, cf. Acts 17.1 ff.). Theirs was a genuine and lasting turning (9, cf. Acts 14.15) and no superficial 'decision' induced by human persuasion.

Such a 'birth' led to outstanding 'growth'. Faith 'showed itself in action' (NEB), their new love 'toiled' in its practical outworking and their hope exhibited 'not the sort of patience which grimly waits for the end but the patience which radiantly hopes for the dawn' (W. Barclay, cf. vs. 3, 10). Further, their lives took on something of the character of Christ and His messengers (6, cf. 1 Cor. 4.16) and they in their turn began to commend the gospel which had been unmistakably imprinted on their lives (7; Gk. *tupos*, translated 'example', was originally used in relation to the impression of a die). All this could not happen without there being an 'overflow', and so it is not surprising that we read that they had become 'a sort of sounding board' (J. B. Phillips) for their faith. Not only most of Greece (the area covered by the Roman provinces of Macedonia and Achaia) but in a seemingly endless variety of other places (Paul uses the word 'everywhere' in hyperbolic fashion), news of their faith had spread (8). Paul found himself unemployed (8)!

We discern here the pattern of all true evangelism. 'A church in every community and thereby the gospel to every creature' was Paul's strategy. Unless we are prepared to take the nature and nurture of local churches with greater seriousness today, our worldwide evangelistic task will continue to be over-weighted with 'professional' missionary endeavour, and thus lose a vast amount of its momentum. How good it is to hear, for example, of Indian believers witnessing widely among their fellow-countrymen and Brazilian churches sending missionaries to Africa!

How much do you pray and work for 'sounding board' churches overseas?

Questions and themes for study and discussion on Studies 49–55

1. What do Luke 10.10–16; Acts 17.31 and Rom. 2.16 teach on man's responsibility in the hearing of the gospel?

2. 'The integrity of mission can only be accounted for by a theology of love' (Douglas Webster). Do you agree?
3. What are the main New Testament principles regarding the relationship of a missionary to newly planted churches?

CHARACTER STUDIES

56: All Aboard

Acts 27.1–15

Luke's vivid writing in this chapter gives us one of the best-told stories of shipwreck in all literature. It is useful to follow a map and imagine the talk, the argument, the apprehensions of this strangely assorted party as the ship's master, under orders no doubt from some Roman shipping firm, risked a late voyage with his cargo of Egyptian wheat for the capital.

The Roman centurion, a man of quiet and effective command, shipped his party in a vessel from Adramyttium, the likeliest craft to put the company into the stream of east-west trade, for Adramyttium lies on the Aegean opposite Lesbos. The vessel had beaten north along the low Palestinian coast, cut between Cyprus and the mainland, as the seasonal winds demanded, and then worked west along the coast of Asia Minor to Myra, at the extreme southern point of the blunt peninsula. Here the party transferred to an Alexandrian cornship, which had perhaps chosen this northern route because of the lateness of the season.

The map at this point reveals the hazards of ancient navigation. The shipmaster made for Cnidus, a port on the south-west extremity of Asia Minor. He was unable to make the harbour, for a wind off shore drove the heavy galley south, and the shipmaster took refuge from the insistent blast under the lee of the 140-mile long island of Crete. Halfway along lies Fair Havens, the port where Paul, one of the most experienced travellers of his age, besought them to stay for the winter—the common practice of ancient mariners. The shipmaster rashly decided to try for another anchorage.

The eastern half of Crete is low, the western quite different. In great heaped terraces, it rises into a group of lofty snow-capped mountains. The old enemy, the north-east wind, funnelled down through the clefts of these highlands, now found them again and drove them off shore round the island of Clauda. The passengers were called in to aid the crew in managing the lurching ship, for Luke remembered vividly the fierce struggle under the brief protection of Clauda to haul on board the boat which was towing water-logged behind.

Danger unites men of diverse character. There were the rugged soldiers, picked men of the centurion's special corps. The centurion himself was a chosen officer in a brigade set aside for special service. Pulling on the same ropes was one of the greatest scholars of his age, the citizen from Tarsus, and Luke the cultured historian and physician.

57: Paul the Leader

Acts 27.16–44

The nor'easter now had the lumbering corn ship in charge. Far to the south, off the African coast, lay the Syrtes, the graveyard of many ships, as underwater archaeology has vividly revealed. Hence the battle to hold a westerly course, aided, it appears by a veering of the wind to the east, as the cyclonic disturbance shifted.

The tremendous gifts of leadership of Paul emerged at the crisis. His advice at Fair Havens had been rejected, and he was human enough to mention the fact, but in Luke's vivid account it is clear that the apostle, not the Roman centurion, nor the captain, was the one who held and stiffened the morale of the company. They were indeed at the end of human resources. They had looped tautened cables precariously round the hull to bind the straining timbers against the stress of the violent seas, and the strong leverage of the mast; they had cut loose and jettisoned all dispensable tackle and gear. And it was all under a murky heaven, with the spray and driving cloud blotting out the stars, and the galley lurching west at nearly 40 miles a day.

The end came. Hearing the sound of distant surf, the sailors suspected land or shoals ahead. The lead showed a shelving seabed, so the hulk was hove to for the night with anchors out astern. This arrangement kept the ship heading in the right direction before the pressure of the still thrusting wind. It was on the fairly transparent pretext of similarly anchoring the bow, that the crew proposed to launch the boat and escape, a plot frustrated by the alert Paul, and a few quick sword-cuts on the ropes at the centurion's prompt orders.

At this point the centurion Julius, or the captain seems to have numbered the ship's complement, a sensible measure before the abandonment of the vessel. They spent the night heaving overboard the cargo of Egyptian wheat, and with the dawn saw an unknown coast, a beach, and a practicable bay. A bar, due to a cross-current, frustrated the attempt to beach the ship which probably drew 18 feet of water, and it was at this point that the escort, who were responsible for their charges, proposed to kill the prisoners. The centurion's admiration for Paul is apparent in the refusal. There was a struggle through the breakers and the whole ship's company reached the beach. It was a triumph for Paul's faith and no small tribute to his dynamic personality.

58: The Centurion

Acts 27.1–6, 31, 43; 28.16; Matthew 8.5–13

The centurion's regard for Paul appears again at Puteoli. We have glanced at this man in passing, but he is worth a closer look. One characteristic of the Roman imperial system, initiated by Augustus himself, was a notable ability to pick men. Even Nero was aided and supported by able ministers like Burrus and Seneca. The army, in important tracts of its history, seemed to produce the most able officers. Lysias was a man of firmness, swift decision and tact, as we have seen, and Paul's centurion maintains the reputation of that class of soldier as they appear in the Eastern command. The Augustan Cohort was itself an *élite* corps, a body of guards, to whom courier and escort duties were committed, and to be a commanding officer in such a regiment was proof enough of fine quality.

He is one of the two centurions whose names we know. He preserved Paul when his men were all for killing the prisoners, as the galley ran ashore. The men, after all, were responsible for the secure delivery of the persons in their charge. In Puteoli, the modern Pozzuoli, the same centurion allowed Paul to lodge with the Christians. It is remarkable that the Christians were so promptly to be found, or that communication between the Christian groups in the Empire was such that the Christians of the busy port were aware of the coming of Paul on such and such a ship.

Paul must have been supremely trusted. This, for Julius, was a much more chancy situation than that off the small island of Malta. The port was big and cosmopolitan. It was full of hiding-

82

places. The Christians were obviously in touch with their brethren in Rome. Rome with its population of a million people was a great warren into which any man could disappear as Onesimus was soon to do. Paul could have been spirited away up the Via Appia with the greatest of ease. It shows courage, acute judgement, and even friendly regard on the part of the senior soldier, to allow freedom.

To be trustworthy as a citizen and a man was a lesson Paul taught. Writing soon afterwards to Philippi, he besought the Church to 'live as citizens worthily of the gospel of Christ' (Phil. 1.27). He was himself a prime example. He had appealed to Rome. He was ready to go there. The centurion duly delivered him to the prefect of the praetorian guards. This was the competent Burrus, who had only two years to live.

59: The Maltese

Acts 28.1–11; 14.8–18

The 'barbarous people', as the AV [KJV] so curiously translates the phrase in v. 2 were the native Maltese, who had watched the galley lurching through the surf. The Greek *barbaros*, of course, simply means those who speak another language than Greek— whose speech, in short, sounds to Greek ears as intelligible as a lamb's bleating (bar-bar). The Greeks called their Persian foes *barbaroi*, while most freely admitting the material superiority of Persian civilization.

Malta had been colonized by Phoenicians ten centuries before Christ. Six centuries before Christ, the island came under the control of the great North African Phoenician city of Carthage which, over the space of a century, disputed the possession of the Eastern Mediterranean with Rome. Hannibal, one of the greatest military commanders of history, was born there. In 218 B.C. Rome took Malta and never lost it. The position, as all history has shown, is strategically vital.

The peasantry of Malta continued to speak their native Phoenician, a Semitic tongue, as closely allied to Hebrew and Aramaic as Arabic is to modern Hebrew. It is not impossible that Paul could make some sense of what they said. Hence the knowledge of what the bystanders thought when Paul, ready as ever to lend a hand at humble work, shook the torpid snake into the

83

fire. This, observe, is Paul's second contact with 'barbarians', or 'foreigners', 'non-Greek speaking people', however it may be translated. He had made a similar impression at Lystra on a Lycaonian community.

The party made itself useful on the island. There is always work for those who look for work to do. The Maltese responded, from the Phoenician proletariat to the 'first man', Publius (Luke again uses the correct term for the chief Roman administrator—it has been epigraphically attested). It is significant, however, in his missionary endeavour, that Paul worked out from a periphery of common culture. The retreat to Lystra was forced on him. Shipwreck landed him on Malta. He planted his Christian cells in points from which diffusion, he hoped, would be spontaneous. He fostered the home base. If semantics made the word for villager (*paganus*) a word for a non-Christian, that was the fault of those who failed to penetrate their country hinterlands.

60: Paul Comes to Rome

Acts 28.11–16; Revelation 17.1–6; 18.9–20

Caught in a web of provincial maladministration, Paul, as we have seen, had appealed to Caesar, and on the chill February day, with the mists from the sea haunting the Campagna, Paul neared the end of his journey. Rome was in sight.

He had long looked forward to that visit. Some ten years before the Christian Church had struck root in the teeming capital, and Paul had written the most difficult and closely argued of his letters to the Roman church. It met no doubt in the house of Hermes, whose frescoed rooms were excavated in 1932. Paul was fascinated by the imperial spectacle of Rome. The great empire straddled the world, netted and tied its parts together with the amazing system of its military roads, policed the far frontiers and held all the strategic points with a firm ironclad hand.

Paul had long since seen that the way to conquest was to meet the might of Rome and the world where it was strongest and most deeply entrenched.

It must have been with eyes of excitement that Paul saw the crumbling monuments and tombs thicken beside the cobbled Appian Way. The smoke and noise of the capital lay ahead, and the traveller had no reason to anticipate anything but justice there. Many more years were to pass before John wrote into the visions of the last book of the Bible a picture of Rome far different from that which occupied the mind of Paul on the cold February morning. The writer of the Apocalypse had seen the great empire turn to persecution, and he pictured her as a woman 'arrayed in purple and scarlet and decked with gold . . . drunken with the blood of the martyrs'.

In February 59 or 60, Rome had not turned on the innocent, and Paul saw that morning the beckoning of opportunity. True, he came a prisoner, when he had hoped to come in freedom, but he may have reflected ironically that he also came at Rome's expense. A million strong, Rome awaited him, and Rome's need was great. The world-weariness of the age was written into the inscriptions he could read on the tombs by the wayside. 'What I ate and drank I have with me,' ran one, 'the rest is lost.' 'Come and have a spot with me,' said another.

South of Rome today there are bits and pieces of the landscape which must be much as they were nineteen centuries ago. The umbrella pines stood then as they do today. So too the pointing candles of the dark cypresses, the dry stone walls, the crumbling, pumicy soil. There are bits of the city rampart which Paul may have seen, grey-green olives, hill-slopes of hungry soil. . .

Paul must have found the challenge daunting and a burden on his heart. Hence the lift of spirits when a band of Christians, alerted by their friends at Puteoli, appeared at the village of Three Shops with welcome.

61: The Praetorians

Acts 28.16; Philippians 1.1–13

Rome's praetorians provided the guard for Paul in his house confinement, and gave him a sphere of evangelism of which we get one glimpse only. It is in the letter to the Philippians, written from Rome. Correctly translated Phil. 1.13 runs: 'It has become clear, through the whole Praetorian Barracks, that it is because I am a Christian that I am in confinement.' The words indicate some wide interest among Rome's household troops.

Augustus had established this special corps in 27 B.C. and half a century later, Tiberius' powerful prefect of the Praetorian Guard, Seianus, concentrated their nine cohorts, till then scattered, into

a single camp just outside the city walls. It was from this dangerous action that the political importance of the Guard and its
commanders dated. They proclaimed Claudius and Nero as
emperors, and sealed Nero's doom by deserting him. They
killed Galba, first of the four emperors to be proclaimed in the
fearsome civil strife of A.D. 68, 69.

Having murdered Galba, the praetorians supported Otho,
second of the four emperors which that year of blood was to see.
They supported Vitellius, who defeated and succeeded Otho, and
were destroyed by a running fight in the streets of Rome and the
final storming of their camp, by the vanguard of the legions which
raised Vespasian to power. Thus was 'the Beast', wounded almost
to death, 'healed of his deadly wound, and all the world won-
dered' (Rev. 13. 3).

These scenes of violence, death, treachery and manifold disaster took place eight or nine years after the final events of Luke's
story. If Paul succeeded in bringing some of the troops to
Christ, they could have been among those involved in the street-
fighting and the battle for the barracks, which were only some of
the incidents of blood and carnage which cursed the whole land
of Italy in the horrible year before Vespasian seized and held
power.

With the changing of the guard at each watch, it could be that,
over the space of two years, half of the 4500 troops in the guard
had some contact with the notable prisoner. It was their day of
opportunity, had they but known it. But that remark passes for
any day. It is quite certain that Paul recognized it and used the
hours to advantage.

62: The Roman Church

Philippians 1.14–30

This passage gives a picture of the church in Rome during Paul's
confinement there. The congregation had been established at least
ten or twelve years before, if the riots in the ghetto at the end of
the forties are to be interpreted as hostility to the Christians. The
nucleus of the church could go back to those who found Christ at
Pentecost. There were Roman Jews among them.

Who then were the group who were proclaiming Christ 'out of

party-spirit, insincerely', thinking to make Paul's imprisonment even more burdensome than it was? He does not seem to disapprove of the general content of their preaching in Rome, so there can hardly have been too much of the Galatian heresy (which laid undue stress on the Law) involved. Magnanimously, though he deplores the spirit of the Roman partisans, he sees a certain propaganda value in their efforts. Perhaps they were the old leaders of the Roman Christians. Corinth is evidence for embryonic sects based on diversity of leadership and teaching. Apollos is evidence for some variety of doctrinal emphasis. So is the first Ephesian church. It is possible that some feared for the future of their teaching, and human nature is tragically prone to treasure a system of thought, and to shun the agony of reappraisement. Pride, too, most pervasive of the mind's faults, enters in, and corrupts even sacred things. Good men took courage from Paul's brightened prospects, and preached Christ from purity of motive. With purpose less pure, others took occasion to establish their own version of the faith, in the absence of the dynamic personality who was confined at Caesar's pleasure. Many a pet doctrine may have been menaced by Paul's authoritative elucidation of the truth. Pet doctrines are difficult to give up, and Paul, a man of conspicuous intellect and learned in three cultures, may not have suffered pretentious error gladly.

It is a little saddening to find the human faults the world knows too well showing themselves so early in the life of the Church, but we have met defective characters already in Acts. It is always well to remember that the Church is not composed of people who are better than the rest, but of people who are seeking by God's grace to be better than they are; not of people who are perfect, but of people who are dissatisfied with their imperfection.

63: The Roman Synagogue

Acts 28.17–31; Romans 3.1–26

Paul's theme in his discussion with the Roman Jews would undoubtedly follow the argument of the letter to the Roman Christians written two or three years before while he was in Corinth. That famous document, to be sure, was for the church, but its very nature reveals the strength of the Jewish section of the community, and the synagogue would be familiar with it, because it would have been the inevitable subject of debate among Jews, Christian and orthodox.

The Jews, according to Paul's consistent policy, had the first chance. They were back in Rome, and obviously Claudius' decree of banishment (18.2) must have been rescinded. Claudius was a learned man, and it could have been his whim to apply what the Athenians called 'ostracism' whereby, without criminal charge against him, a person was asked, for the good of the city, to leave for a period of ten years.

In consequence, if some attempt is made to see matters from the point of view of the Roman rabbis, it is fair to concede that they had their difficulties. Nero had succeeded Claudius, and during the first five years of his principate, that pleasure-loving youth left affairs largely in the hands of the competent Burrus and the wise Seneca. If one or both of these men was instrumental in allowing the Jews to return, it would have been on condition that they keep the peace. A phrase in Suetonius suggests that the earlier banishment had been because 'of Christ', or 'Chrestos' as the historian's garbled information had it some seventy years later.

And now a notoriously controversial figure had arrived, one whose path through the eastern and central lands of the Mediterranean had been strewn with riot and disorder. Or so, at least, the career of Paul could be represented by the timid and the cautious, not to mention the openly hostile. No Jew cared to have his hard-pressed community wantonly disrupted. Reception, in consequence, was mixed (24), and Paul set before them the honoured words of the great Isaiah. We are allowed to be present at the last interview when, with some severity, the apostle announces again his 'turning to the Gentiles'.

64: Characters of Acts

Colossians 3

Glance back at the host of people we have met in Luke's book. The Christians of its thirty years of story would make a typical congregation for any church. They range from the servant girl Rhoda to the brilliant intellectual Paul. They include the physician

Luke, the business-woman Lydia, the jailer of Philippi, two synagogue heads, a member of Athens' most sophisticated judicial body, an Ethiopian cabinet-minister, a country-boy from Lystra, two tent-makers from Rome, a lame beggar from Jerusalem, a Cyprian landowner and a strong-headed young man who quarrelled with an elder.

They came from a dozen cities Jewish, Greek, Roman in race. They were far from perfect, for on their periphery were sly deceitful folk like Ananias and Sapphira, scamps like Simon, and charlatans like the sons of Sceva. Their enemies ranged from Herod the king to the Sadducees and Pharisees of the Sanhedrin, the head of a trade-guild and the rabble of the market-place. Their message was received with yells of rage and the throwing of stones, with the polite deferment of Stoics, the mirth of Epicureans, the fear and self-seeking of one Roman governor and the impatience of another, and the irony of a well-informed king. (In spite of a once well-known hymn, Agrippa really said: 'In short, you think to make me a Christian?' Paul's reply was a play on words: 'In short or at length, no matter, but I could wish one and all here stood where I stand—save, of course [ruefully said] these bonds.')

There is a fine picture of the Empire at work—the magistrates, men of cool integrity like Gallio, anxious like Festus, calculating, and taking risks with peace, like Felix. One can sense the atmosphere of Palestine, moving forwards to the great explosion. There were the lesser levels of authority, functioning smoothly, the Asiarchs of Ephesus, the Areopagus of Athens, Lysias and the Jerusalem garrison . . . It is almost 'a conducted tour' of major cities of the Graeco-Roman world, as a leading modern historian has recently remarked. We see the crowds, the minorities, the majorities, the sects, the denizens of the streets. It is the same world today, the same men and women, the same Church—fortunately it is the same Christ.

Questions and themes for study and discussion on Studies 56–64

1. Luke as a reporter.
2. Paul's leadership. On what did it rest?
3. The centurions of Scripture.
4. Equality on the beach.
5. Rome in Paul's strategy.

6. Paul's concept of opportunity.
7. The old congregation and the newcomer.
8. Absorbing controversial figures.
9. What have you learned in Acts?

THE MISSION OF THE CHURCH

Paul the Missionary

65: Called by the Spirit

Acts 13.1–12

Paul had received early notice of what his life's mission was to be
(**22**.15, 21; **26**.16 ff.; Gal. **1**.16). Barnabas, with his large-hearted
capacity for the work of God, recognized in him a man of God
with considerable spiritual potential, and brought him to Antioch
(**11**.23–26). Together, they taught the new believers there. Barnabas and Paul were among the gifts Christ had begun to give to the
Antiochan church (1, cf. 1 Cor. **12**.28 ff.; Eph. **4**.11) and during
the course of one of the leaders' seasons of worship (accompanied
by fasting to encourage greater spiritual earnestness, cf. **14**.23)
the Holy Spirit exercised His ministry of selection and direction
for the work of the gospel (2). It is probable that the will of
the Spirit was made known through the utterance of one of the
prophets, who, with his colleagues, expressed the oneness of the
church in the new venture by a further period of waiting on God
and in the laying on of hands (3, cf. **6**.6). In this way, they were
'let go' by the church and 'sent out' by the Spirit (3 f.). 'The world
ministry which thus began was destined to change the history of
Europe and the world' (E.M. Blaiklock).

There are a number of ways in the New Testament in which
God through His Spirit disperses His servants in order to spread
the gospel. Sometimes, He uses the uncomfortable events of
persecution (**8**.1, 4; **11**.19 f.); at other times, individual guidance,
apparently unrelated to fellow Christians (**8**.5, 26, 39 f.). But when
it comes to someone closely linked in service with a local church
fellowship, He ensures that the church itself is not only aware of
what He is doing but is linked in full sympathy (cf. **16**.1 ff.). There
are times when it is right for individual Christians not to 'confer
with flesh and blood' (Gal. **1**.16) in finding God's will; but what
a tragedy when this becomes the practice of young people in
local churches interested in missionary service!

Paul's first recorded encounter as a missionary with paganism bore the characteristics of much that was to follow: forthright proclamation of the evangel (5), interest and response (7, 12) and full-faced opposition (8 f.). The pattern has not changed over the centuries!

What does your church know of the voice of the Spirit in relation to the service of its members (2)?

66: Emboldened with the Word

Acts 13.42–14.7

The three major features of Paul's ministry which emerged at the end of the last study are seen more clearly in today's section. We see firstly the *forthright proclamation* of the divine message, called variously 'the word of God' (13.44, 46, 48, 49), 'the word of His (God's) grace' (14.3) or simply 'the gospel' (14.7). The 'subjects' (13.42, NEB) on which Paul spoke were the mighty accounts of God's deeds in Israel's history (13.16–41) in which the God of Abraham, Moses and David was clearly identified with the God and Father of Jesus Christ who now offered men forgiveness of sins (13.38), and eternal life, 'the life of the age to come' (13.46, 48), an age which in Christ had now dawned. The very certainty of the message conditioned the manner of presenting it (cf. the 'boldly' of 13.46; 14.3). Neither hint of apology nor quiver of fear do we discern. These were men under commission (1 Cor. 9.17), ambassadors for the living Christ (2 Cor. 5.20), and were wholly taken up with their task.

In the second place, we notice the *fierce opposition* that such preaching aroused. This came initially from the Jews (13.45) and then, at the instigation of the latter, among various sections of the community at large (13.50; 14.2, 5). It took on a variety of forms ranging from open contradiction and the reviling of the message (13.45) to a poisoning of personal attitudes (14.2) and hostile acts of rejection (13.50; 14.5). The Jews not only reacted against the actual message but were no doubt thoroughly aggrieved at the way Paul so easily drew away the 'Gentile worshippers' (13.43, NEB). Once more, however, we notice how God makes the wrath of man to praise Him through causing persecution against His people to become a means for the wider spread of the gospel (14.6 f., cf. 8.4; 11.19).

The third leading characteristic of the witness both of Paul and the Early Church was the *fruitful consequences* evident in the conversion of men and women. In contrast to the blatant opposition of the Jews was the eager responsiveness of the Gentiles to whom he subsequently turned (**13.**42, 44, 48), and the fulfilment of Isaiah's prediction regarding the world-wide ministry of Christ (**13.**47; Isa. **49.**6) was marked by that abundant joy already noted wherever men have received the gospel (**13.**48, 52, cf. 1 Thess. **1.**6).

Is part of the reason why we do not see more of features two and three today found in our weakness on feature one?

67: Caring for the Churches

Acts 15.36–16.10

The relatedness of all of Paul's ministry to the founding and nurturing of local churches is nowhere more evident than in this passage. His 'Come, let us return ...' (36) was spoken in full remembrance of the fierce treatment he had previously received in those same regions of Asia (e.g. **14.**5, 19). His ministry of 'bringing new strength to the congregations' (**15.**41, **16.**5, NEB) was effected in two ways: through his personal ministry of teaching, and his presentation of the guidelines drawn up by the apostles and elders at Jerusalem (**15.**23; **16.**4). It was typical of what was to follow throughout his life, not only during his subsequent missionary journeys (e.g. **20.**2, 17 ff.), but also through the medium of his writings, which were basically not evangelistic documents but Bible teaching 'letters to young churches' (J. B. Phillips). Much of the work of overseas missionaries today is involved with just such a 'nurturing ministry' among younger churches. The strategic work of those engaged in such spheres as Bible College teaching or lay leadership training must be viewed every way as important as that of the more 'traditional' jungle pioneer or rural doctor.

To fulfil his task of preaching and teaching, Paul needed colleagues. He himself had once been chosen by Barnabas (**11.**25) and had soon become the senior partner (note the change from 'Barnabas and Saul' in **11.**30; **12.**25, etc., to 'Paul and Barnabas' from **13.**43 onwards). Now came *his* turn to select, and the first occasion was not an entirely happy affair (**15.37 ff.**). Paul's personal judgement (cf. **38**, NEB) led to 'a sharp clash of opinion' (**39**, J. B. Phillips) which led to 'a parting asunder', 'an uncommonly strong expression (E. M. Blaiklock). Unlike Barnabas, Paul was not prepared to wait for men to develop into greater maturity but looked for more 'instant' reliability and effectiveness. Paul had no doubt taken note of Silas' character both during the journey from Jerusalem to Antioch and during Silas' ministry there (**15.22, 32**), and chose him accordingly.

In the event, the division between Paul and Barnabas resulted in a wider spread of the gospel (**15.39–41**), and it is good to read of Paul's subsequent esteem of Mark's usefulness in Christian service (2 Tim. **4.11**). Paul's selection of Timothy (**16.1 ff.**) was much more straightforward, particularly as the young man was commended by the Lystran church (cf. 1 Tim. **1.18**; **4.14**). Thus, continually directed by the Spirit (**16.6 ff.**), Paul moved on with his colleagues in glad obedience to the unfolding pattern of God's call to him (**16.10**), carrying his 'daily . . . responsibility for all the churches' (2 Cor. **11.28**; J. B. Phillips).

Do you 'care' enough for young believers?

68: Preaching to the Greeks

Acts 17.16–34

When Paul arrived at Athens, he could remain no mere onlooker when confronted with the hundreds of temples and pagan sculptures that 'filled' the city (**16**). What he saw with his eyes made a sharp, spiritual impact within him (**16**), and this in turn prompted him to positive action (**17 f.**), a very commendable sequence indeed!

He was met with a level of opposition and unbelief that he had rarely encountered in his previous ministry: the 'professional philosophers' of the Athenian debating circle who wished to pick the brains of this supposed 'cock sparrow' of an orator (**18**, J. B. Phillips). The amazing ability and versatility of Paul's trained mind (cf. **22.3**) are seen very clearly in what proved to be 'Paul's first major exposition of the gospel to an audience without a background of Old Testament theology or Jewish thought' (E. M. Blaiklock).

It is important to see that Paul did not set out in the first place to identify their 'unknown deity' with the one, true God he knew (23). Rather, he declared his intention of announcing to them the truth about God in view of the fact that they had, in this open way, confessed their ignorance about it. Paul went on to affirm some of the great truths about God, His creatorship (24), His self-sufficiency (25), His sovereignty over, and design for, man, all planned so that man himself should respond to Him in worship (26 f.). In relation to this theme Paul goes on to quote two extracts from Stoic poetry dealing with the Greeks' devotion for Zeus, 'considered ... the Supreme Being of Greek philosophy' (F. F. Bruce), readily acknowledging that even in the midst of pagan thought, there are some glimpses of truth to be found. As he moves to the major thrust of his sermon, however, Paul makes the issue abundantly clear. Man must put aside all his pretensions and projections about ultimate reality and the sort of 'god' he imagines to be 'there', and repent and believe in the risen Son of God, the Judge of all (30 f.).

No worship, outside the Hebrew-Christian tradition of God's revelation as contained in the Old and New Testaments, can possibly be truly satisfying to man or acceptable with God, however sincere it may be. Man may grope and grasp for God, but because of the devastation within him caused by sin (Rom. 3.9 ff.), he can never truly find Him. *Only in Jesus Christ is the true meeting point to be found*, and in all dialogue and encounter with men of other faiths, this must be the centre of the Christian's message, even as it was Paul's.

'Paul was not a man to take a complete holiday from the main business of his life' (F. F. Bruce). How often do you?

69: Engaging in the Conflict

2 Corinthians 10

Relationships between Christian workers and those among whom they minister are of major importance in the work of God, and Paul undoubtedly had his full complement of problems in this realm! Some of the believers at Corinth accused him of a divided approach (1) and worldly motives (2) and, consequently, of a lack of authority to teach them (8). In the midst of misunderstandings and suspicions like these, Paul realized that only an approach modelled on that of his Lord would prove adequate (1). On the one hand there must be 'gentleness' (NEB, the Greek word means basically 'strength under control' cf. Matt. 11.29) and 'magnanimity' (NEB, the Greek word signifies the exercise of justice tempered with love and understanding as well as exactness cf. John 8.1–11). On the other hand there must be a blend of firmness and consistency (2, 11, cf. Matt. 21.12 ff.; 23.13 ff.). This is always the right way forward for Christian workers involved in similar situations.

Together with these 'internal battles', Paul was faced with the major 'external' battle against the entrenched strongholds of evil in the hearts of men (4 f.). He knew that behind the 'sophistries' (5, NEB) and 'every towering obstacle erected to prevent men from knowing God' (W. Barclay) was the activity of the Evil One whose purpose and work it was both to blind and bind men in unbelief (cf. 2 Cor. 4.4; 2 Tim. 2.26). He realized that such activity could only be confronted and defeated by spiritual means (4, cf. Psa. 20.7; Eph. 6.12 ff.), a truth that Christians today need to bear firmly in mind. With so much importance at the present time being placed in human organization, prowess and resources, whenever the Church forgets the essentially spiritual nature of the battle in which she is engaged, impotence and defeat come upon her immediately.

In the midst of such battles, Paul knew himself to be a man under divine direction, with limits of service clearly demarcated for him (13). He realized that God was the great Commander of operations for the advance of His Kingdom among men, and if all His servants were obedient to Him, there would be no overlapping (14 f.). The challenge of the 'lands beyond' (16) was ever on his heart (cf. Rom. 15.20). He knew, however, that to venture further afield without properly fulfilling the initial task God had given him, i.e. the building up of the faith of the newly born church (8, 15), was to court the superficial.

Obedience to the Divine Commander leads both to victory and effectivenes in Christian service. How obedient are you?

70: Protesting for the Truth

2 Corinthians 11

Paul was the founder of the Corinthian church (1 Cor. 4.15; 2 Cor. 10.14) and consequently felt a particular burden of responsibility for its healthy development and doctrinal purity. He was continually aware of the dangers of invading viruses and parasitic growths that would damage the church's well-being (cf. Acts 20.29 ff.; Phil. 3.2), and he was faced with this very danger at Corinth through the activities of 'sham-apostles' (13, NEB) who were preaching 'a different gospel' (4, Gal. 1. 6ff.) and masquerading under the guise of being true teachers of God's Word (14 f.; Matt. 7.15). Such men were 'courting' those whose love was intended to be 'single hearted' for Christ, and in doing so were the very instruments of Satan (2 f.).

While having no desire to parade his own credentials, Paul knew that the growth of the young church and the truth of the gospel were at stake. Thus, he urges the Corinthian believers to consider two main aspects of his ministry. Firstly, the sources of his financial support (7–11) surely indicated to them that he was not out for mercenary gain. He had a right to 'earn his living by the gospel', being supported by the free-will offerings of those to whom he ministered (cf. 1 Cor. 9. 3–18); yet at Corinth he had been supported initially through his own tent-making work (Acts 18.1 ff.) and later by gifts from other churches (8 f.). This was the only 'robbery' he had committed among them (8)! In the second place, there were the incontrovertible marks of the manner of man that he was and what preaching the gospel had meant for him in terms of suffering and risk to life itself (22–33). His Hebrew upbringing (cf. Phil. 3.5), the extent and hazards of his evangelistic ministries and finally, in contrast to these 'external things' (28, NEB), the inward burden of love he carried for the young congregations which demanded unreserved and sympathetic self-giving in all situations (28 f.), were surely sufficient evidences of the genuineness of his ministry. Paul called God Himself to witness to the veracity of such details (31). 'There has been no inaccuracy and no over-statement' (R. V. G. Tasker).

For world mission, mastery of the language, adoption of new customs, and exertion of abundant energy are all needed; but a man's or woman's ministry stands or falls in the end by the quality of their life.

97

In the long term, no 'outward show' can hide the true nature of inward quality. How genuine is your service?

71: Captured by the Gospel
Philippians 1.1–18

The outflow of Paul's life for the progress of the gospel (12) stamps these verses. Paul writes to a church that he had been instrumental in founding (Acts **16**.12 ff.) and nourishing (Acts **20**.1 ff.), and which had developed sufficiently both to appoint its own leadership (1) and to partner him in the work of the gospel (5). His dominant concern is for their continuing growth in life and character, in a love that was not blind but 'full of knowledge and wise insight' (9, J. B. Phillips). He longed that they might both aim for and attain the highest in holy living (10), showing the evidences of the presence of the risen Christ within them (11, cf. John **15**.4 ff.; Col. **1**.10). 'His heart throbbed with the heart of Christ' (J. B. Lightfoot, 8) in a pulsation that was expressed through the twin channels of Christian instruction and prayer (4, 9, cf. Col. **1**.9 ff., etc.). That Paul could in this way maintain his ministry to those from whom he was separated is inescapable evidence of the supreme quality of his own love and care for them (cf. **4**.1, etc.).

Were he to have been in the quiet of a 'missionary residence' at the time, such warm, earnest writing would have been quite understandable. But he was held in a Roman prison (12), chained to the leg of one of his captors (13, the word 'praetorian' could indicate the emperor's palace in Rome or the headquarters of a district governor). In such circumstances, love could not be bound, and neither could the gospel itself, as Paul himself gladly goes on to testify (12–14). This was not the only time when Paul had cause to glory in the 'unchainable' gospel (cf. 2 Tim. **2**.9) and even though the preaching of it was undertaken at times with mixed motives (15–18) as long as 'Christ is set forth' (18, NEB), there could be few grounds for despondency.

The gospel can break out of every circumstance, and the measure to which it does so is a measure of the Christian's spiritual maturity and effectiveness in service.

'In prison . . . Paul was as much on duty as the guards who were posted to watch over him' (*R. P. Martin*).

72: Setting out the Standard

1 Thessalonians 2.1–16

As Paul reflects on the abundant worthwhileness of his visit to Thessalonica (1), some of the leading characteristics of his apostolic ministry shine forth. In all that he suffered (Acts **16**.19–24), Paul exhibited a divinely given *courage* that caused him to declare the gospel 'frankly and fearlessly' (2, NEB). In contrast to the activities of the wandering street orators of the day, his preaching was with *integrity*, devoid of deceitful or debased motives (3, 5). His presentation of the evangel centred in a thoroughgoing sense of *responsibility* in relation to the 'gospel of God' (the phrase occurs three times in vs. 2, 8, and 9 and by inference in v. 4) with which he had been entrusted (cf. Gal. **2**.7; 1 Tim. **1**.11). In a spirit of *selflessness* (6), he held back from insisting on proper standing and rights as an envoy of Christ (cf. 1 Cor. **9**.4 ff.; 2 Thess. **3**.9) but gave himself as a father to his children in a *compassion* that expressed itself in gentleness (7) and carried the individual with it (8, Gk. *psuchē* 'selves' denotes here the whole personality rather than 'a body-entombed soul', a concept quite alien to the Scriptures). 'It is still true that vital Christian service is costly' writes Leon Morris. Not for Paul a path of ease, whether this implied the laborious toil (a strong Gk. word) and fatigue (9) of *hard work* or an uncompromising life of *godliness* (10; the three words Paul used in relation to his holy living stress religious devotion, legal rectitude and moral purity respectively, cf. **1**.5 f.). Only such a quality of life could commend the *care* he showed for the believers' spiritual development (11 f.).

Let no one underestimate the demands made on those who are called to minister in the name of Christ whether it be among men of a similar or dissimilar culture. Only Christ can give the strength sufficient 'for these things' (2 Cor. **3**.5 f.).

How much does your life show the above seven characteristics?

73: Building up the Faith

1 Thessalonians 2.17–3.13

To proclaim the gospel is one thing; to see this gospel being clothed effectively with renewed humanity is another. It was the latter desire that constituted Paul's longing to be assured of the Thessalonian believers' spiritual health and growth. He is concerned primarily about the stability of their 'faith', a word mentioned no less than 5 times in this passage. This was an obvious focus for Satan's attacks (3, 5) just as his own movements were proving to be at that time (2.18; cf. Acts 17.8; 18.6, 12). These young believers were the fruit of his missionary activity, the joyous and glorious evidences that he had not served his Lord in vain (2.19 f.); and news of their firm stand in the gospel made all the difference to his daily living (8 f.).

If Paul 'feared' for them (3.5), it was because he realized the danger of their becoming discouraged by the opposition they were encountering on account of their Christian profession. It was not that he had not warned them of the inevitability of such (4, cf. Matt. 5.11 f., Acts 14.22; 1 Pet. 4.12 f.) but real-life encounters always bring their own unique challenge however much careful preparation there has been beforehand. In any event, suffering for Christ was seen to be an essential accompaniment of following Him. 'What had been an acute problem to faith in Old Testament times—the suffering of the righteous—had come to be recognized as an essential element in God's purposes for His people' (*New Bible Commentary*).

The chief means of nourishment for faith in such circumstances is a ministry of establishing and exhortation (the latter verb is the one derived from the word 'Counseller' or 'Comforter' in John 14.16, 26, etc. cf. Study 36), and the one who was sent to fulfil it (3.2) returned with the glad news of the fruit of it (3.6). With the bright expectation and implication of the return of Christ particularly in view (2.19; 3.13), Paul prayerfully anticipates the Thessalonians' further progress in love and holiness (12 f.) through the direct ministry of the Lord Himself and, eventually, he trusts, through himself (11).

Wise parental care and an adequate, balanced diet are essential prerequisites through a child's early years if strong effective adulthood is to be realized. This is as true in the work of God among men as it is in the child-care centre!

Have you a 'Timothean ministry' (3.2) to fulfil with someone or some church?

Questions and themes for study and discussion on Studies 65–73

1. 'In all the four instances, then, of sending out Barnabas, Saul, Silas and Timothy, what the New Testament emphasizes is *not* the initiative of the individual . . . but always the initiative of others . . .' (Michael Griffiths). What practical application does this have to missionary recruitment today?

2. 'Many of us today are intellectually embarrassed to speak of the lostness of the lost' (Francis Schaeffer). Why is this so?

3. How can the strategic nature of caring for growing and developing overseas churches be better understood and appreciated when the work of the 'jungle pioneer' continues to make such strong traditional appeal in local churches today?

CHARACTER STUDIES

74: Paul's Humility

Romans 1.1–17

This beautifully written introduction reveals much of Paul.
Rome was one of the goals he sought, for the strategy of his
evangelism, as we have seen, was world-wide. He had planted
churches in key towns of the eastern Mediterranean. He now
looked to Italy and Spain, and Rome was his essential base of
operation. It was the heart of empire, and if ever there was a
place in which Paul's theory of radiation applied it was in the
great city on the Tiber. There had been a church in Rome for over
ten years, and Paul had no thought of by-passing its witness or
dispensing with its aid, although he must have known how
much such beginners in Christ, with no New Testament to guide
them, needed his help and instruction. We have guessed some of
the pain certain members of that community were to cause him.

Humility is the teacher's best gown. Read again vs. 9 to 12
to see how Paul wears it. 'I long to see you,' he says. 'I want to
bring you some spiritual gift to make you strong; or rather, I
want to be among you to receive encouragement myself through
the influence of your faith on me as of mine on you' (11 f.,
NEB). He owed a debt, he said, to people of all nations, for
'Greek' must be understood to contain the notion of Roman and
of Jew, and 'barbarian' was simply 'foreigner', as we saw in the
case of the Maltese islanders. It is the common way of man to
imagine that life and the world at large owe a debt to him. The
Christian, bought by grace to serve, should have no such mis-
conceptions. Paul never did. He is writing to a young church
which he had no hand in founding. He is writing with the
immense prestige of established and proven leadership. He was
accepted as 'the apostle to the Gentiles'. And yet no arrogance,
no unnecessary assumption of authority, mars the graciousness of
his approach.

Said John Ruskin: 'I believe the first test of a truly great man
is humility.' And Sir Thomas More: 'To be humble to superiors,
is duty; to equals, it is courtesy; to inferiors, is nobleness; it being

102

a virtue that, for all its lowliness, commands those it stoops to.'
Such was Paul's leadership. He was a great soul.

75: The Romans

Romans 1.18–32

Paul's picture of a godless society can be illustrated from a
century of Roman poets, satirists and historians. Paul was writing
during the principate of the young profligate, Nero, when
Roman society was sunk in hideous vice. It has been left to the
present day to produce again on the stage the nude and open
sexuality which scandalized the more sober writers of Nero's day.
Petronius, so ably portrayed in Henryk Sienkiewicz' historical
novel *Quo Vadis*, was writing, at about the same time as Paul, a
piece of fiction which has partly survived. It concerns the base
doings of three Greek scamps in the sea-ports of Campania, and
is dark confirmation of all Paul here writes. Anyone who seeks
evidence in support of the apostle's grim description can read
Petronius' *Satiricon*, Seneca's *Letters*, Juvenal's *Satires*, Tacitus'
historical works, and Suetonius' *Lives of the Caesars*. Paul was
writing to dwellers in Rome, some of them 'of Caesar's household' (Phil. 4.22), who had all this before their eyes.

Paul was, in fact, describing a doomed society, and much of
what he writes hits too shrewdly home for comfort in the 'per-
missive society' of today. No nation was ever destroyed from
without which had not already destroyed itself from within.

In a little-known speech of January, 1838, Abraham Lincoln
put the thought well. 'At what point,' he asked, 'shall we expect
the approach of danger? By what means shall we fortify against
it? Shall we expect some transatlantic giant to step the ocean, and
crush us at a blow? All the armies of Europe, Asia and Africa
combined could not by force take a drink from the Ohio, or
make a track on the Blue Ridge, in a trial of 1,000 years . . .

'If destruction be our lot, we ourselves must be its author and
finisher. As a nation of free men, we must live through all times,
or die by suicide.'

The words retain notable relevance in Lincoln's own land—and
in many other lands—almost a century and a half later.

And what is society but the sum-total of its members? It is
evil men and women who build an evil society, and no community

103

can be organized and legislated into good. A society, a people, a land, are what individuals make them by faith, their virtue, and their justice, or by their base surrenders, their lack of reverence for God or good, and by the evil choices of their secret thoughts.

76: Paul's Learning

Romans 2

The personality and character of a man, as we have had more than one occasion to remark emerge from what he writes, especially when he writes to persuade, with a cause hot in his heart. We meet Paul, the rabbi and the Jewish scholar, in this chapter, and then pass on to encounter Paul, the Hellenist, skilled in Greek debate, and appreciative of the best in Greek philosophic thought.

Verse 11 is a key verse, the thought of which Paul characteristically expands. The possession of the Law, he maintained, here and always, carried a heavy responsibility. The incredible sophistries of the scribes angered Paul. Some of them actually quoted: 'If you will diligently hearken . . .' as a proof that doing took second place to hearing. With Paul, as with James, it was no true faith which did not demonstrate its reality in conduct. The Pharisees, to whose school Paul belonged, were clear enough on this point. They regarded doing, not merely learning, as 'the Leader', that is, the guiding precept in any division of their code. It is interesting to see, in the easy flow of his argument, how familiar Paul was with the fashion of such theological debate.

But not every Pharisee could have passed with Paul's versatility to the continuing discussion, which any Greek would have recognized. Anyone with a sensitive ear for that irony which is so characteristic of cultured Attic writers, will recognize it in the last dozen verses of this chapter, as they will in the first four chapters of Paul's letter to the Corinthians. Paul's knowledge of the Stoics, the noblest school of philosophy active in the world of his day, was obvious, as we saw, in his address to the Athenian court.

It is also visible in the central verses of this chapter of close and urgent argument. The Stoics had a doctrine of a law written on the heart. They were the first Greeks to use the word 'conscience' in a Christian sense. Aristotle, too, before the Stoic school was founded, had written: 'The truly educated man will

104

behave as if he had a law within himself.' Sophocles, in his noblest play, five centuries before Paul, had made Antigone tell the tyrant that there were 'unwritten, irrefragable laws of heaven' which could not be broken. Paul moves with graceful ease through these tracts of thought.

77: Paul and the Law

Romans 3

The Stoics, who invented preaching and the sermon, often taught by setting up an imaginary objector. Paul follows their method in this chapter. Indeed, he could have had a real objector in mind when he speaks of those who took and twisted his doctrine of grace to make him say that the more we sin, the more God has to forgive, and the more wondrous the benison of His grace—a fiendish perversion in Paul's estimation (8).

But the agony of his soul lies behind much of what follows. He was a Pharisee. He had revered the Law. Could the Law then do nothing? Was it a vast and sterile failure? In long brooding in Arabia, after he came to Christ, Paul had come to see the truth, that the Law set standards which, in his human strength, man could not keep. The Law, therefore, convicted of sin, and stressed the need of a Saviour and salvation by grace.

In the whole chapter, Greek though the shape of the dialectical argument may be, Paul speaks as a Jew, using, as Christ used, the accepted and honoured words of the Old Testament, to prove that, for all who had eyes to see, this truth had always been clear. There is a rapid-fire quotation, which was called a 'catena' or 'chain', in which verse follows and reinforces verse, to one irrefutable end. It was characteristically rabbinical, and in such debate the context of a quotation was not always of prime importance.

But return to the blasphemy, as Paul would describe it, of the argument advanced, sometimes libellously (8), in the opening verses. It is not so remote from later heresies as might at first sight appear, and Paul gives us an inkling with what sort of rapier logic he would deal with much of our modern decayed theology. I have written elsewhere: 'By one means or another, by diminishing man's responsibility or by misrepresenting God, man, the sinner, seeks to avoid the admission, in all heinousness, of his sin. The modern theologian, compromising with "permissiveness", murmuring excuses about "situation ethics", speculating on God's "involvement" in the world, and avoiding the Bible's downright condemnation of sin, has no cause to be impatient with his ancient counterpart.' (*The Daily Commentary* [*Bible Study Books*]—*Romans*).

78: Paul's Peace

Romans 5

At the beginning of ch. **6** Paul is to return briefly to the distortion of his gospel which had so shocked him (3.8), but meanwhile he breaks into a fine passage on the fruit of faith in the life. Like so many parts of this intense letter, it is obviously biographical, and an expression of what had been given to him in the stress of experience.

His conversion had ended one conflict. He gave in, and kicked no longer, like a maddened ox, against the goad. Then came the mental conflict of discovering the meaning of the Old Testament and the Law. But underneath the intensity of his thought and the labour of his daily living, was the peace beyond all understanding. It was the peace which came to his troubled soul when he realized that he was justified by faith, that the battle was over, and the calm which he could by no means win through obedience to the impossible standards of the Law, was his by the grace of God. The rebellion was finished. The soul which was at odds with God was accepted by God's action. Peace once made, the reconciled sets out, as Paul set out, to become the sort of person God intended him to be.

God is available (2). Nothing bars the way or alienates, and faith becomes, not only the act of appropriating salvation, but a daily pattern of life. Hence victory over anything life can do. Paul never said, and no one ever should say, that Christianity is easy. No one had a more trouble-strewn path than he. But trial and tribulation, he had found, committed in faith to the wise, transforming hand of the Almighty, produced rare qualities of character. The endurance, of which Paul speaks, must be seen in the context of his whole life. It is no crouching under the shield of faith while adversity hurls clanging down every missile in its armoury. The shield could be a weapon of offence, and Paul's endurance was active. Hence character (4). No sturdiness forms in a hothouse. The English archer made his most trusty arrows out of the wood which grew on the side of the tree exposed to the north. Hope grows from this, and no man lives joyously without hope. God is real to the surrendered life—a theme Paul is to resume in ch. **12**. And hope is real, because faith makes God real. This is what his faith had taught Paul.

79: The New Paul
Romans 6; 7.15–25

Paul was acutely conscious that he was a new man in Christ. He was utterly convinced about the resurrection of the Lord. He makes that clear enough to the Corinthian church which contained a faction prepared to regard the doctrine of the risen Christ as a species of symbolism, a myth, if the oddly abused modern term is to be used. To Paul it was historic, proven fact.

At the same time, he thought of the death and resurrection of the Lord as a mystical experience in his own life. He had died with Christ at baptism, and risen from the water as though coming back from burial to a new life altogether in which old ways withered, and new vigour surged.

And yet, such is the daily experience of Paul and of any one of us, that such a condition demanded the unbroken nurturing of faith. The 'old man', a brilliantly imaginative conception of Paul, was alive, and struggling for dominance against the 'new man', brought to birth by faith. It requires daily exercise of faith to 'reckon' old urges dead (11), and to promote and further every thrust and aspiration of the soul towards good and God, by the continual infusion of trust and ready belief. It is a reorientation of all thinking and desire.

Such was the pattern of his living. Plato, in a famous dialogue, had taught something similar under the myth of the two horses of the charioteer we call the soul. The dark horse dragged downwards, the white horse strove gallantly upwards, and it was the task of him who held the reins to make them pull together. Both Plato and Paul were psychologically sound. Paul never strikes a more universally audible note than when he talks of this strange strife within the personality.

Paul knew that life was conflict, and that the nature of man slips easily towards evil. Those who teach otherwise deceive

107

themselves and those whom they teach. The Bible sets no limits to the Christian's victory over his baser self, but it can lead to nothing but frustration and despair to suggest to those who come to Christ that all sinlessness lies effortlessly within the reach, and to give the impression that there is no strife, no temptation, no chance of defeat save in unbelief. Paul never taught this, for he knew better. His words at the end of ch. 7 are no mere recollection of unregenerate days. They arose from his daily experience.

80: Paul's Testimony

Romans 8.31–39; 2 Timothy 1.12

We have not read all of ch. 8. This letter is commonly read for the doctrine it contains and that is set forth for Scripture Union readers in *The Daily Commentary* (*Bible Study Books*) on the epistle, and in many conservative commentaries. We need not here look again at the often misused doctrine of predestination and its reconciliation with free will. We seek the man behind his words. We are looking for Paul, and how can he be better revealed than by allowing him to utter his ringing testimony in his own words. He is about to begin a detailed exposition which occupies three chapters. It is a characteristic address to the synagogue. He concludes ch. 8 with a moving paragraph. Paul had a gesture. He 'stretched forth his hand' (Acts 13.16) and began to speak. The RSV does not do justice to the passage. The NEB and Phillips are better. But let him speak in a completely new translation:

'In view of these things, what then shall we say? If God is on our side, who is against us? Since He did not spare His own Son, but gave Him up for all of us, how shall He do other than in grace, along with Him, give us everything? Who shall lay a charge against those whom God has chosen? God, who counts them righteous? Who condemns? Christ?—He who died, more, rose again, who is also at God's right hand, who also pleads on our behalf?

'Who shall part us from the love Christ bears us? Shall trouble, the pressure of life, persecution, deprivation of food or clothes to wear, danger, violent death? (The word says: 'For your sake we face death all the time. We are considered sheep to be killed'). But in all these things we win more than victory through the One who loved us; for I am utterly convinced that neither death nor life, neither beings of another world nor powers or authorities in this, neither what is here present, nor what yet is to be, neither what is above nor what is below, nor anything else created shall be able to part us from the love of God shown us in Christ Jesus our Lord.'

These words are no idle words. They are the words of a great soul and proven in the fires of life. He suffered under every head. They killed him, and, were he here, might kill him again, so fragile is good, freedom, the rule of law. The words are true, and in them we meet the man. Let us hearken.

81: The Committed Christian

Romans 12

In these character studies we have looked at characters that are, and characters that ought to be. Romans 12 tells us what the Christian should look like. Let us read the first two verses, translating the first verb in the sense in which a modern Greek would take it. He uses 'I beseech' (*parakaleo*) as 'Please'. Probably it meant that in Paul's day. And so; 'Please, brothers, in the name of God's mercies, dedicate your bodies as a living sacrifice, consecrated to God, well-pleasing to Him, which is the worship proper to your nature.

'And cease trying to adapt yourselves to the society you live in, but continue your transformation by the renewal of your mind, to the end that you may test out for yourselves the will of God, that namely, which is good, well-pleasing to Him and perfect.'

This crowded chapter which so reveals the writer's yearning soul and is to cover every phase of Christian living with detailed precept and exhortation, begins with an appeal to the most compelling of motives. God's compassionate dealings with man never failed to stir the wonder of the one-time rebel and persecutor of the Church. It appeared to Paul, and it has appeared to every true follower of Christ from then till now, that it was an obvious duty to respond to God's love with all the poor means in man's power. Forgiven much, Paul gave much.

Man has a body, the instrument and vehicle of his spirit. Let him take it, and all that goes with it, and 'place it by the altar'. In one of his passages of grand eloquence, which we have recently read, Paul has already said something like this: 'So sin must no longer reign in your mortal body, exacting obedience to the body's desires. You must no longer put its several parts at sin's disposal, as implements for doing wrong. No: put yourselves at the disposal of God, as dead men raised to life; yield your bodies to him as implements for doing right . . .' (Rom. 6.12 f.).

A Christianity which did not penetrate and interfuse the activities of the body, daily living, business, social life, the human person, in all its actions, reactions and common tasks, was not, in Paul's view, Christianity at all. He returns thus, from the loftiest flights of theological instruction to the human situation as it confronts every man. With a new outlook, a cleansed purpose to guide and determine action, members which might easily become the tools and weapons of evil can 'glorify God' in a new service. That service finds its first occasion and expression in ordinary life. Christian citizenship is the Christian's first duty, and Christian citizenship begins in complete surrender of the person to God.

Read this 'character study' in several translations, and set it beside performance.

Questions and themes for study and discussion on Studies 74-81

1. The importance of city-based Christianity. What of the future?
2. 'No nation was ever destroyed from without, which had not already destroyed itself from within.'
3. Unwritten laws. Have you any?
4. The importance of authoritative Scripture. Can evangelism function without it?
5. Faith, committal and character. How are they linked?
6. How is 'the old man' weakened?
7. Can we make Paul's testimony ours?
8. 'Adapting ourselves to the society we live in.' What are the limits?

THE MISSION OF THE CHURCH

Motive for Mission

82: Sharing Good News

2 Kings 6.24–7.20

The four lepers (7.3) were faced with an agonizingly difficult choice. Conditions inside the beleaguered city of Samaria had reached starvation level (6.25) even to the point of cannibalism (6.28). To stay in the 'no man's land' situation at the city gates was equally hopeless. The only prospect of survival was in a show of mercy on the part of the hostile Syrians (7.4), not a very bright possibility. However, they followed this gleam of hope (7.5), leaving the forlorn Israelites shut up to despair behind them, and entered into an unbelievable experience of deliverance and abundance (7.7 f.). The contrast between the city gate and the Syrian camp could hardly have been more amazing!

In the midst of their immeasurable enjoyment, they suddenly realized the responsibility that was theirs in relation to those who were as equally needy as themselves yet still unaware that such bounty was available (7.9). A sense of shame and guilt overtook them as the essentially selfish nature of their actions broke upon them. Inaction and delay were put aside, and with a 'come, let us go and tell . . .' they moved off to share the 'good news' of their discovery with others.

The joy of personal experience and the inescapable sense of obligation to share the reason for it with others blend to form a dominant motive for Christian witness. The believer testifies to that which he had 'heard . . . seen . . . looked on and touched' (1 John 1.1), a principle that finds a practical outworking in numerous New Testament situations (e.g. John 1.40–46; 4.28 ff.; 20.18 ff.). This desire to witness should be irrepressible (Acts 4.20) even amidst opposition (Acts 5.41; 8.4).

Of course, people take some convincing at times! The inhabitants of Samaria were full of incredulity at first when they heard of the miraculous deliverance that God had provided for them (7.12 ff.). 'It's too good to be true!' is the often repeated remark (cf. John **20**.25) when the Christian tells of God's wonderful grace revealed in Jesus Christ. But the evidence is there to be investigated and verified (7.15) and, in the last resort, men and women have only themselves to blame if they wish to remain imprisoned in a city where death is the only prospect (John **3**.36).

*Does the injunction of 1 Pet. **3**.15 find you basically lazy?*

83: Indebted to Men

Romans 1.1–17

Paul knew that his ministry as an apostle of Christ and as a spokesman for the gospel was not the result of a personal choice but of a divine commissioning (1, cf. 1 Cor. **1**.1; **9**.17). The scope of this mandate embraced men and women of 'all nations' (5) and he thus found himself under a sense of obligation in preaching the gospel to them (14). Among the Gentiles his potential hearers were of very mixed quality indeed. On the one hand, there were the educated and civilized Greeks, whom many regarded as having no need of further enlightenment; on the other, there were the ignorant and rough-hewn Barbarians who were usually set aside as completely beyond the bounds of any moral improvement. But Paul knew that both groups stood in equal need because of their common 'sinnership' before God (Rom. **3**.19, 23). He knew that it was only through the gospel that the power of God was available for the overthrow of evil and the establishing of righteousness in the hearts of men whoever they were and wherever they were to be found (16 f.). 'Paul was their debtor not by any right that either Greeks or Barbarians had acquired over him but by the destination which God had given to his ministry towards them' (R. Haldane).

Of course, this gospel which had God as its author (1) and Christ as its focus (3, 9) met with widespread rejection wherever it was proclaimed. The Jews met it with hostility because of its claim to supersede the Law and to identify Jesus as Messiah. The Gentiles met it with contempt because to vaunt death on a cross as a triumph of any sort was deemed to be plain stupidity (1 Cor. **1**.23). Despite all this, Paul was proud to testify to the power of the gospel in his own life and to tell it forth unashamedly

(16). He gloried in the Cross (Gal. 6.14), and the desire to make its message known among men impelled him ever forward (15, cf. 2 Cor. 10.16).

How up to date are you in the repayment of your spiritual debts to your fellow men?

84: Proclaiming Salvation

Romans 10

In spite of all that he had suffered for the gospel's sake from his fellow-countrymen, Paul's practical and prayerful concern for their salvation was irresistible (1). It sprang from his firm understanding of the uniqueness of God's work of grace in reckoning men guiltless before Him on the grounds of the death and resurrection of Jesus Christ mediated to them by their act of personal faith (4, 9 f.). No human grouping had preferential treatment from the One who was ready to give His grace in abundant measure to all who called on Him (12 f.). No major exertion was needed to bring this salvation within reachable distance (6 f.); 'Christ is ever available to faith and so likewise is the gospel' (*New Bible Commentary*). It grieved Paul that the Jews, of all people, could display such 'unenlightened zeal' in expending their energies on a way of living that could never bring them into a right relationship with God (2 ff.).

From the major principle of 'salvation in Christ alone', there arose the major corollary that men had to hear the good news first of all in order to have an opportunity to believe it, and for them to hear it, messengers were needed to proclaim it (14). This commitment of God to human instrumentality is both awesome and yet eminently reasonable. The gospel contains spiritual truths presented in an ordered and intelligible manner. In order to receive the benefits Christ waits to bestow, men must know who He is, what He has done for men and what they, in turn, must do to receive His salvation. What better way to hear than through those who have come to know these truths in their own personal experience? Certainly, the possibility of believing in an 'incognito Christ' or finding Christ as Saviour through sincere religious questionings within a non-Christian religious system such as Hinduism or Buddhism, while attractive speculation, hardly squares with the nature of the gospel or the nature of man as a rational, responsible being.

If men can only be saved through response to the Christian gospel, then it must, with all speed, be taken to them by human messengers and it is apparent that this urgency was one that gripped Paul throughout his missionary activity. Certainly, his feet moved swiftly to 'preach the good news' (15, Isa. 52.7) even if those who were best prepared to receive it proved uninterested and unresponsive (18, 21). The responsibility of 'the watchman' is basically unaffected by the response of those to whom he declares his warning (Ezek. 33.1 ff.). His part is to 'blow the trumpet' and 'warn the people'; theirs is to 'turn and live' or face the inevitable alternative.

How much urgency is there in your Christian witness?

85: Stewarding Responsibly

1 Corinthians 9.13–27

Few other passages in the New Testament reveal so much of Paul's motivation in mission as this one. He declares first of all that although he had every right, as a minister of the gospel, to be supported by the voluntary offerings of those who benefited from his teaching (13 f.), yet he preferred to preach 'without expense to anyone' (18, NEB). His motivation lay not in the expectation of sizeable financial reward from a job for which he had personally opted (17), but in response to an inner compulsion which 'bore in' upon him (16; note the use of the verb 'to lay' in such verses as Luke 5.1 where it is translated 'pressed' and Acts 27.20). He was a man under divine appointment (cf. Study 83), committed to a task of responsible 'stewardship' (the root meaning of the word 'commission', 17). In the Graeco-Roman world, a steward was a person called to a right use of that which had been entrusted to him by another (1 Cor. 4.1 f.) and for Paul this meant the effective sharing of the grace of God with men (Eph. 3.2, 7 f.). This responsibility lay in two directions: towards God, whom he served and whose gospel he proclaimed (1 Tim. 1.11), and towards men, who stood in such need of this gospel and to whom he had been sent (Acts 26.17). Individual patterns of involvement will vary, but such stewardship is held by every

Christian, for it arises out of the very nature of the gospel itself.

The message of God's grace so gripped Paul that in order to win men for Jesus Christ, he was ready to go to any lengths necessary within the bounds of his Christian commitment (19 ff.) and without compromising the gospel itself (cf. Gal. 2.11 ff.). He likened his manner of living to that of an athlete who needed to maintain optimum physical fitness and single-heartedness of purpose for the event for which he was entered (24 ff.). The race was there to be won and the opponent in the ring there to be hit (26)! If such purpose and concentration could characterize the sportsman, Paul reasoned, how much more should the Christian bruise his own body and 'make it know its master' (27, NEB) to serve his Lord acceptably. With the context of the whole passage being 'service' rather than 'salvation', Paul's fear was not that he might finally be lost—he knew that for him, as for all true believers, this was impossible (Rom. 8.29 f., 38; Phil. 1.6, etc.)—but that if he neglected his own 'spiritual fitness', God might have to set him aside in preference for others who were more usable.

How 'spiritually fit' are you for Christ's service (1 Tim. 4.7)?

86: By Love Constrained

2 Corinthians 5.10–21

The knowledge that he was answerable to a divine tribunal (10) produced in Paul a humble and obedient reverence before God (11). This, in its turn, led to a purposeful attitude to others as he 'addressed his appeal' (cf. NEB) to them regarding the gospel by which they also one day would be judged (Rom. 2.16; 1 Cor. 4.5). A purely dispassionate approach to men with the gospel, embodying 'a take it or leave it' attitude, is quite alien to the pursuance of Christian mission. 'Proclamation' inevitably involves 'persuasion' (cf. Acts 18.4; 28.23) in that person to person encounter in which God Himself is the major Spokesman (20).

Whatever interpretations were put on his ministry (13), Paul knew that his inner motivation was the love of Christ (14). It left him 'no choice' (NEB) and we see the force of the Greek verb in such verses as Luke 8.45, 12.50, and Acts 18.5. The love that moved Christ to have compassion on the multitudes (Matt. 9.36–38) and to touch and heal the leper (Mark 1.41) moved in

Paul's life and moves today in the lives of all who would serve Him, unerringly channelling their actions to others.

Paul had reflected much on this love and had reached firm conclusions (14, NEB). He saw that it embraced 'all'; that 'innumerable company of those who would enjoy the benefits of redemption' (R. V. G. Tasker). He knew that it resulted in newness of life (17, Rom. **6**.4) and a restored relationship with God (18 f., Rom. **5**.1, 10). Genuine compassion is always grounded in truth and the more this truth is understood, the wider will be the personal experience of the love of God. In this passage, we see a very clear blending of experience and theology, which both shows the dependence of the former on the latter and the inevitable connection between the two. When we try to divorce them, mission becomes distorted and troubles begin to multiply!

*How far have you begun to plumb the dimensions of the love of Christ (Eph. **3**.18 f.) ?*

87: Completing the Course

Acts 20.17-38

A race is entered to be finished and won despite all the obstacles and dangers that may be encountered while running it. This was the imagery in which Paul saw the ministry he had 'received from the Lord Jesus' (24). He knew himself to be a man under divine commission (1 Tim. **1**.1, 12) and the passion to bear testimony to God's grace dominated his life (24). To effect this ministry with the required humility (19) and perseverance (31) had involved him in a rigorous sequence of suffering (19, 23), hard physical effort for the support of others and himself (34) and a self-giving that cost him emotionally (31) as well as in every other way. Even life itself was held lightly in comparison to the completion of his task (24, cf. Phil. **1**.20; **2**.17). Through it all, there was a resolute teaching of the Word of God in which he did not flinch from presenting any part of God's truth that, while initially appearing unsavoury to the hearers, was needful for Christian venture (20, 27). Nor did he withhold those centralities of the gospel which, though frequently despised by men, comprised the essential steps to salvation (21, cf. Acts **17**.30; 2 Pet. **3**.9).

The ministry of Christ was characterized by a similar perseverance that refused to be dimmed or diverted by seemingly more attractive alternatives (Matt. **4**.8–10; Luke **9**.51; Heb. **12**.2) and embodied that tenacity of purpose that had already been prefigured in the person of the Servant of the Lord (Isa. **42**.4. See Study 12). Such was the quality that stamped Paul's life and made him righteously yet compassionately indignant about those who had been deluded into surrendering a once firmly held strong intent to follow Christ (Gal. **5**.7; 2 Tim. **4**.10, cf. Matt. **19**.20 ff.).

The men and women who have made their lives count for God are those who have pressed forward with singleness of purpose despite discouragements and temptations to give up. After the disastrous fire in Calcutta in March, 1812, that destroyed many of Carey's manuscripts and large stocks of paper, he could write: 'I wish to be still and know that the Lord is God . . . He will no doubt bring good out of this evil.' 100 years later, C. T. Studd, chided at leaving his home and family at the age of 52 to preach Christ in Africa, replied, 'If Jesus Christ be God and died for me, then no sacrifice can be too great for me to make for Him.' Of such fibre are men of mission made.

*Have you learned how to endure with patience and joy (Col. **1**.11)?*

88: Anticipating the Finale

Revelation 5.1–14; 7.9–17

'The Revelation' is a book of anticipated glory, and an integral part of this glory is the culmination of God's redeeming purposes in the perfecting of His Church. Throughout history, God has been choosing a people to bear His Name among the world's peoples (Acts **15**.14, NEB). It is His purpose that this great company should, as part of the riches of its salvation, share in a fellowship of mutual love and service which, while only imperfectly realized during life on earth, will be perfectly attained thereafter. Through the acclamation of the enthroned Lamb, firstly by the four living creatures and the twenty-four elders (**5**.8) and then by a vast concourse gathered before that heavenly Throne (**7**.9), John is given a vision of the redeemed of all ages drawn from all segments of human settlement on earth. This multitudinous throng is seen clad in white robes (9), 'perfect in the righteousness of Christ' (L. Morris), and destined to share in a triumphal rule (5.10). Exegetes may wish to identify the two groups of chapters 5 and 7 in different ways, according to which school of biblical interpretation they support, but the above noted characteristics are certainly common to all God's glorified people in every age.

No turn of history or assault of evil can sway God's purposes for the perfecting of His Church (Matt. 16.18; Rom. 8.28–30), and the end of the world will only be ushered in when the last of God's people is brought to a saving knowledge of Himself through faith in His Son. To some, this may appear to paralyse missionary effort; for if this is God's irrevocable purpose, then will He not accomplish it regardless of the obedience of His people? The contrary, however, is the case. 'Instead of rendering evangelism superfluous, election demands evangelism. All of God's elect must be saved. Not one of them may perish. And the gospel is the means by which God bestows saving faith upon them. In fact, it is the only means which God employs to that end.' (R. B. Kuiper).

In the knowledge that Christ's Church is being built among 'all nations', then, the servants of God can set their faces to their world-wide task with much expectation, awaiting both their Master's return (Luke 12.36) and the perfection of the Church in which, by God's grace alone, they themselves will share (Luke 10.20).

Does the biblical doctrine of the Church breed complacency or concern in your life?

Questions and themes for study and discussion on Studies 82–88

1. 'Our supreme need is not a new strategy of mission but a new inspiration for mission' (Douglas Webster). How accurate an analysis is this?
2. What is involved today in being 'put in trust with the gospel' (cf. 1 Thess. 2.3 f.; 1 Tim. 1.11; Titus 1.3)?
3. Illustrate from Scripture and contemporary life the main reason for lack of adequate perseverance in Christian service.

CHARACTER STUDIES

89: Paul the Citizen

Romans 13.1–10; 1 Peter 2.13–17

The chapter contains several echoes of the words of Christ. Paul must have been very much aware of matters yet to find their written form. Paul was to tell the Philippians, themselves, many of them, Roman citizens to 'live as citizens worthy of the gospel' (Phil. 1.27). He now speaks as one who sought to do so, and in so doing reveals much of himself.

It is important to see Christian society in the first century in proper perspective. The Empire, running to the Rhine, the Danube and the Black Sea, and bounded to the west by the Atlantic, and to the south and east by the great deserts, had given the Mediterranean world a stable peace. The Roman Peace was the social and political framework within which the Christian Church attained its first international form.

Roman history, written from the standpoint of the aristocratic writers of the capital, inevitably concentrated on Rome itself, on the vices and doings of the court and the prince, ignoring the proletariat and the provinces. It is historic fact that, during the principate of the youthful Nero, whose vice and profligacy became legendary, the provinces enjoyed such quietness and stability that 'Nero's Five Years', the quinquennium during which government was largely controlled by the wise Seneca, and the soldierly Burrus, became a legend of just administration throughout the Roman world.

Paul had learned in Gallio's court, and he was to learn again in riotous Jerusalem, that Roman discipline and justice, rough though it sometimes was, and corrupt though it could be in such vicious hands as those of Felix, was a protection and a shield. Moreover, the Jews were restive throughout the world. The mood of the Empire's most difficult people was heading towards the tragic explosion of A.D. 66, and that event had world-wide repercussions. As Paul found when seeking a passage from Corinth to Jerusalem, and again in Jerusalem itself, a collaborating

Jew such as he was, with his assumption of Roman citizenship, was in acute danger.

He was also, perhaps, hopeful that the fabric of the Empire could be christianized, and he did not wish the Church to become branded as a dissident, rebellious group. A decade later Rome drove the Church into this position, but hope of partnership still lived when Paul was writing. The Empire, too, was sensitive about organizations within its body.

90: Paul in Uniform

Romans 13.8–14; Ephesians 4.22–24

Let this touch of Paul's poetry (in vs. 12 to 14) mingle with the testimony of a great Paulinist, Augustine of Hippo. In spite of the word picture of v. 12, the concluding verse of the chapter would seem to speak of clothes. J. B. Phillips translates: 'Let us be Christ's men from head to foot . . .' and Conybeare: 'Clothe yourself with Jesus Christ . . .'

This was Augustine's famous text. Augustine and his friend Alypius were in Milan where, under the counsel of the great Ambrose, they had turned to the study of the Epistle to the Romans. One afternoon the pair were sitting together in a garden in a suburb of Milan. The roll of the apostle's letter lay on the seat between them. Augustine was in his thirty-second year, deeply concerned over a wasted life, and obviously in a state of serious tension. Something in the letter moved him to tears and wild lamentations. He rushed from Alypius and fell weeping under a fig tree in a far corner of the garden.

Now let him tell the story: 'So I was speaking and weeping in the bitterest contrition of my heart. And look! I hear a voice from our neighbour's house, a boy's or girl's I know not, chanting repeatedly: "Pick it up and read, pick it up and read." Suddenly with changed countenance I began with the most concentrated thought to consider whether children were accustomed in any sort of game to chant anything like this, nor could I at all remember having anywhere heard the like. Checking my rush of tears, I rose with no other thought in mind than that here was God's command to open the book and read the first chapter I should come upon . . . So I hurried back to the place where

120

Alypius was sitting, for there I had put the book of the apostle when I got up. I seized it, opened it, and read silently the first section on which my eyes fell: "Not in revelry and drunkenness, in debauchery or vice, nor in quarrelling and jealousy, but put on the Lord Jesus Christ and take no thought for the flesh and its appetites." I did not want to read on. I had no need to do so' (trans. E.M.B.).

The figure is a vivid one. Clothes cover, protect, envelop, preserve, like the 'grace which covers all my sin.' But more than this. Is it not a fact that the clothing of man or woman is the first impression their presence makes upon us? Before any word has revealed a personality, the outward appearance has confronted our sight. Face and features vie with the clothing of the body to make an impact on the mind.

When Paul repeated his figure of speech in the letter to the Ephesians (4.22–24) he sharpened this point. Phillips has caught up his meaning well; 'No, what you learned was to fling off the dirty clothes of the old way of living, which were rotted through and through with lust's illusions and . . . to put on the clean fresh clothes of the new life which was made by God's design for righteousness and the holiness which is no illusion.' So Paul hoped to do.

91: Paul's Plans

Romans 15

Observe the graciousness with which Paul writes. He now takes the Roman Christians into his confidence about the future. He has travelled arduously and long. Christian churches were strewn along his path. He tells us here of journeys about which we know nothing—the journey into Illyricum, for example. Whether he ever reached Spain, the western province of the Empire, we do not know. It was an important project. Only a few remains of Latin literature are in our hands from the fifties and the sixties of that century, and most of it is the work of Spanish Romans. Seneca, Nero's tutor and prime minister, his nephew Lucan, the epic poet, and several others prominent in Rome's contemporary cultural life, came from Spain. Spain was also to provide three emperors, including Trajan and Hadrian.

It was a brilliant piece of strategy, to set his eyes on the great Iberian peninsula, and if Paul failed in that well-planned objective, it was because of the visit to Jerusalem, and the arrest which followed the unwise advice of the church domiciled there, so timidly anxious to reconcile its narrow-minded Pharisaic wing (Acts 21).

At the same time, such is the creative power of God, out of that tragic misadventure came the 'prison epistles' and perhaps the two books of Luke. Paul was no man to see other than a second opportunity in the thwarting of his plans. Denied one alternative, Paul took another, and found himself flung into the midst of a pattern of Gentile evangelism which he had not envisaged.

He went opened-eyed into the danger which he knew lurked in the capital of Judaism. Read closely for the poignancy of their autobiography the four closing verses of the chapter. He asks them to pray for his deliverance from the most vicious anti-Christian group in the world, and that his demonstration of Gentile goodwill might find acceptance with the reluctant Christians of the Jerusalem church. Neither prayer received the answer he sought, but out of the denial God brought unmeasured good. Such is the lesson of Paul's fate. And another lesson: consider the scope of his evangelistic plan along with the meagre resources with which he undertook it. And ask whether we, with distance annihilated, and a world of science and technology at our disposal, can proportionately match it.

92: Paul and the Women

Romans 16.1–8; Galatians 3.28; 1 Corinthians 11.12

The passages above are a clear enough indication that Paul was no misogynist. In the word to the Corinthian church listed in the readings, there is a touch of poetry, for does he not mean that, though Gen. 2.23 speaks of woman taken from man, since then, without woman, man could not be born?

In the greetings to the Roman church, of whose personnel Paul seems to have had the most detailed information, out of the twenty-five people in the full list about one third are women. Of the eight mentioned specifically by name, only two lack comment. The other six all have some word of warm and appreciative regard. Priscilla, now back in Rome from Corinth and Ephesus, along with her husband, 'risked their lives' for Paul. Mary 'worked hard' for the Christians. So did Tryphaena and Tryphosa, who seem to have been twins. William Barclay points out the whimsicality of Paul's commendation. The meaning of their names was 'Dainty' and 'Delicate'. The verb for working hard was *kopian*, a participle of which is used of the Lord sitting wearied on the kerb of the Sychar well (John 4.6). It suggests that the sisters' toil belied ironically their tender names.

We meet again Phoebe of Cenchreae, a woman of substance, who seems to have journeyed to Rome to deliver the letter. She is honoured with the title of 'deaconess'. Junias, as the RSV puts it, appears in versions which follow another textual tradition, as Junia, and the name was probably feminine. She is, to be sure, called an apostle, and this was accepted as early as John Chrysostom in the fourth century.

The list is therefore eloquent of Paul's regard for the women connected with the Church. He also believed, and most people would agree with his conviction as biological and psychological fact, that the sexes differ, that there are, in general, tasks for which women are better fitted than men, and other tasks for which men are commonly better fitted than women. In a smoothly functioning Christian community, such division of labour falls into proper place without tension or rivalry. Paul has been misunderstood, mainly by the defensively belligerent, over women and their place in life. His regulations should be read and examined only in the context of his life.

93: The Rest

Romans 16.9–27; Mark 15.21

Many of the names listed here appear in contemporary documents. Some of them are of special interest. Narcissus was one of the two freedmen (Pallas, Felix' brother was the other) who acquired a corrupt and dangerous influence over the emperor Claudius. Narcissus amassed a fortune, and had great political power. After Claudius was feloniously poisoned in A.D. 54, he was arrested and driven to suicide. His household, however, servants, professional staff, and the hundreds of skilled men such a minister would gather round him would continue, though absorbed into the vast imperial family, to function as a coherent whole.

So too with the household of Aristobulus. It seems likely that Aristobulus was the grandson of Herod the Great. Claudius, a conscious imitator of Augustus in his foreign policy, had fostered the Herodian house, and it is known that Aristobulus was educated at Rome, and given a 'household', that is a staff, by Claudius. At Aristobulus' death, this body would be absorbed also by the imperial *familia*, but, in the interests of administrative efficiency, would be preserved as a separate unit. Apelles (Abel), and Herodion, mentioned before and after the group, were probably members of it.

It is quite clear that Christianity was penetrating high circles in Rome. Whether Nereus is another indication is a matter of conjecture. Nereus certainly, a generation later, was a high official in the household of Domitilla, grand-daughter of Vespasian, who married Titus Flavius Clemens of the same imperial family. She became a Christian as did also, it seems, her husband. Clemens was executed by the base Domitian, last emperor of the Flavian house, and Domitilla banished. The cemetery of Domitilla, on the Via Ardeatina outside Rome, was used for Christian burial in the first century, and the name of one Nereus was connected with it. There is no evidence to prove that the Nereus of this list is the same person, caught in the apostolic reference at an earlier period in his life, but it is intriguing to think that he, freedman or slave, could have been the entry-point for the faith into a household so exalted.

And is Rufus possibly the son of Simon who bore the cross for Christ? Conjecture, to be sure, but these 'characters of the Bible' were living men and women, serving the Lord a few years before the grim date in July A.D. 64 when Rome went up in flames, and Nero, seeking a scapegoat for what was probably his own crime, fell upon the Christians.

94: Caesar's Household

Philippians 4

While we are meeting the Christians of Rome, so soon to be the harried victims of Nero's hate and panic fears, we might turn to a

124

greeting Paul sent from Rome two or three years later, when he was in house-confinement there awaiting the hearing of his appeal to Caesar.

He underlines a greeting from Caesar's household. It would seem likely that he found much help and alleviation of his lot by the contact he obviously had with Christian and Jewish members of the staffs of Narcissus and Aristobulus, who, on the decease of their household heads, had become a part of the imperial 'family'. It seems likely that the 'household of Caesar' (Phil. 4.22) was, at least in some part, composed of these two earlier groups into which the Christian faith had penetrated early in its Roman history. They probably formed the strength and nucleus of the church in Rome when Claudius banished the Jews from the capital in A.D. 49, and, as the emigration of Aquila and Priscilla to Corinth shows, swept a Christian minority along with them.

This infiltration appears to have been maintained. Tertullian and Dionysius of Alexandria both speak of considerable groups of Christians in the imperial household, and it has recently been pointed out by Professor G. Clarke of Melbourne that certain surviving Latin inscriptions, which mention 'the one God', and 'brethren', common Christian expressions, could be epitaphs of the church. One inscription mentions a school on the Caelian Hill which was staffed and equipped to train administrative officers for the imperial civil service.

'Caesar's household' means precisely the imperial civil service, not the palace slaves, so here is evidence that, early in the history of the Church, the faith had formed a bridgehead in the most influential levels of the Empire. We know nothing more, but it is obvious that Christians so entrenched were in a position to exercise incalculable influence.

Scripture tells us nothing more. We should be glad to know these pioneers of the gospel, and it is possible that archaeology may yet have fragments of information to add to the little we know. But why did Paul say that it was principally those who were of Caesar's household who sent their salutations to Philippi? It was easier to answer the question when it was thought that the members of Caesar's household were poor and deprived slaves, who had shared Paul's gifts from Philippi. This appears to be far from the truth.

Questions and themes for study and discussion on Studies 89–94

1. How should a Christian exercise his citizenship today?
2. 'Putting on' Jesus Christ. The word picture of clothing.
3. The second opportunity of thwarted plans. Failure as a path to success.
4. Women in the tasks of the Church.
5. The social spread of Christianity today. Does it affect all classes?
6. The strategy of Christian infiltration. Is it available still?